Fairy Tales from Everywhe

Uniform with this edition

Fairy Tales from Here and There
Fairy Tales from East and West
Fairy Tales from Near and Far

Other Fairy Tale collections by Amabel Williams-Ellis
Arabian Nights
Fairy Tales from the British Isles
British Fairy Tales
More British Fairy Tales
Grimm's Fairy Tales
Fairy Tales from Grimm
More Fairy Tales from Grimm

Fairy Tales from Everywhere

Retold by

Amabel Williams-Ellis

Illustrated by William Stobbs

Blackie
GLASGOW AND LONDON

Acknowledgements

The Publishers gratefully acknowledge permission to use copyright material granted by the following: Angus and Robertson Ltd for 'A Legend of Flowers' ('No Flowers') and 'Gayardaree or the Duck-billed Platypus' ('Biggoon and the Little Duck') from *Australian Legendary Tales* collected by K. Langloh Parker; Routledge and Kegan Paul for 'The Story Spirits' from *Folk Tales of Korea* collected by Professor Zong-in-sob; George G. Harrap & Co. Ltd for 'The Monkey Bride' ('Little Pet Rani') from *Hindu Fairy Tales* by Dewan Sharer.

ISBN 0 216 90257 6 (hardback)
ISBN 0 216 90256 8 (paperback)

Blackie and Son Limited
Bishopbriggs, Glasgow G64 2NZ
450/452 Edgware Road, London W2 1EG
Printed in Great Britain by
Robert MacLehose and Co. Ltd
Printers to the University of Glasgow

Contents

No Flowers

LONG AGO in Australia, when the Great Spirit had made the world and everything in it, he went away to live in a far-away heaven. High, high was his heavenly camping-place, far above the tops of the great Oobi Oobi mountain. But alas, when he went, the flowers that grew among the grasses of the plains, the flowers that grew on the dry stony ridges and the flowers of the trees, all drooped and withered, so that the earth seemed suddenly desolate and dreary, and children were born to the tribes who would never see a flower.

The older people used to tell them tales about how there had once been these lovely things, blue, red, yellow, white or purple, shaped like stars or a cupped hand, and that they were gay as parrots and sweet-scented. The children, who had never seen such things, found these tales hard to believe.

It was no good for the women to go into the bush with their bark dishes. There was now no honey that they could collect. True, they could find sweet saps and gums that ran down the branches of the trees when the black ants had been gnawing the twigs higher up. These saps were sweet, like maple syrup, but they were not as sweet or as scented as honey, and there was nothing now on earth as lovely as the flowers.

At last the wisest men of the tribes decided that however long the journey might be they must try to travel to the camp of the Great Spirit. When they got there they would beg him to make the earth beautiful once more, as it had been when they were young. They did not tell the tribes where they were going, but one day, before sunrise, these men set off, travelling north-west.

The journey was very long, across wide plains and over stony ridges but, after many days they saw in front of them the great Oobi Oobi mountain. It seemed that this mountain was so high that the sky rested on its top. They went near and began to walk all round the base of it, but the mountain seemed to be one great rock that rose so steeply that there was no place on its sides for a man's foot to lodge.

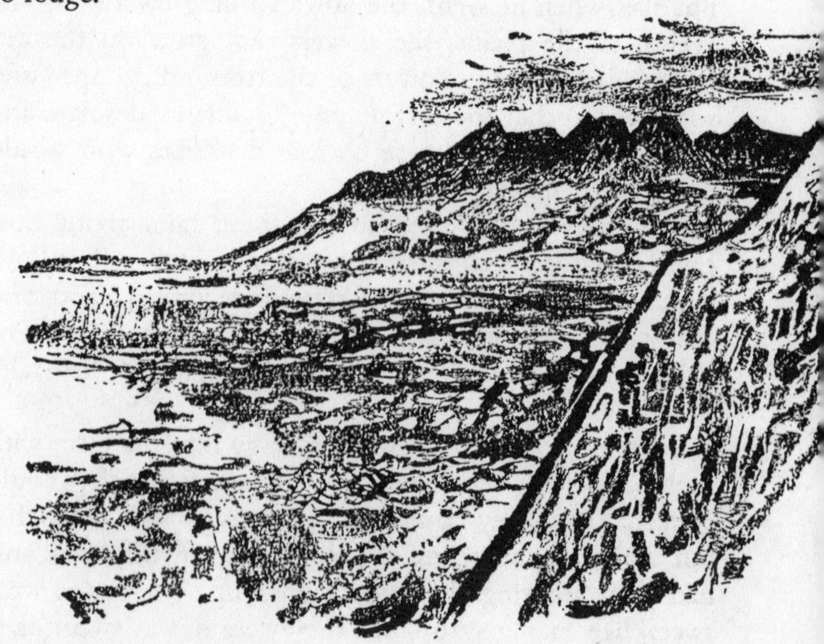

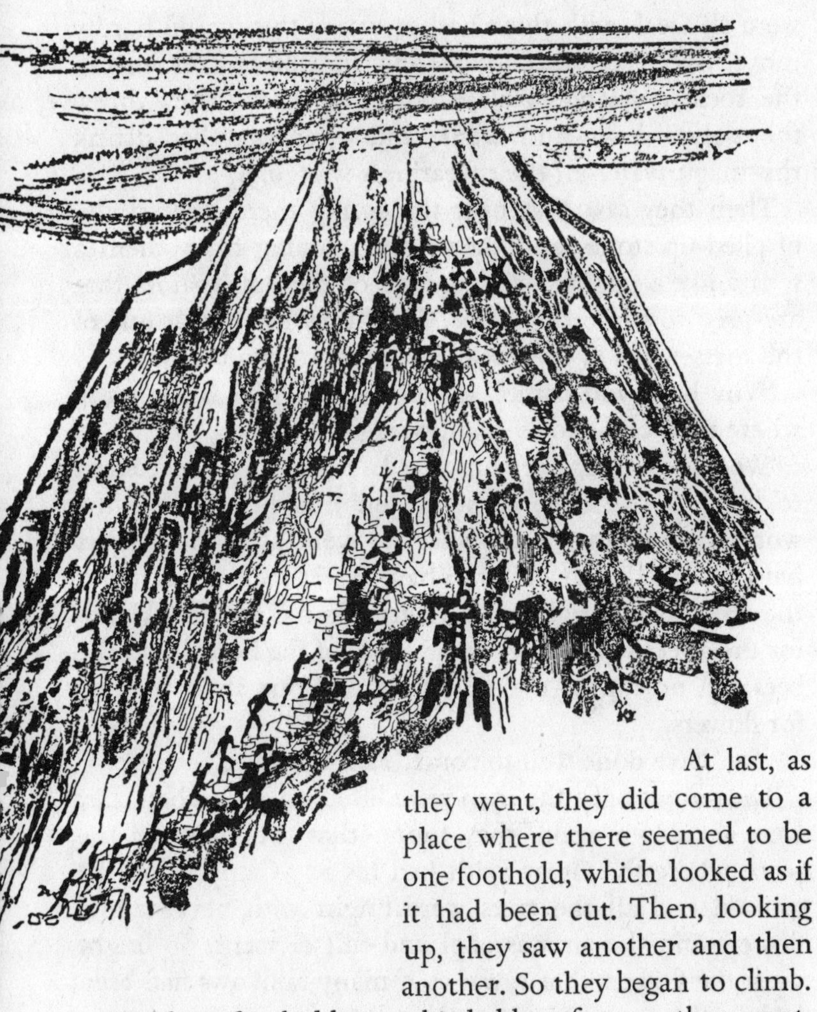

At last, as they went, they did come to a place where there seemed to be one foothold, which looked as if it had been cut. Then, looking up, they saw another and then another. So they began to climb.

Up these footholds, up this ladder of stone, they went. They climbed all one day, but the top of the mountain seemed no nearer. All the second day they climbed and all a third. Still there were footholds, each a little higher than the other.

At last on the fourth day, coming round a steep shoulder of rock, they found that they were at the top. By now they were all weak with thirst and so weary they could hardly move. Great was their joy to find, in a place hollowed in the rock, a spring of clear bubbling water. They threw themselves down and drank, and when they had drunk this magic water all their weariness was gone.

Then they saw that near the spring there were circles of piled-up stones and they heard coming from them a sound like a mighty wind or one of the bull-roarers that are used to summon a tribe. Then they knew that one of the messengers of the Great Spirit was calling them.

'Why have you come?' asked a voice. 'This is the place where men come to seek knowledge.'

'We have come,' they answered, 'to beg the Great Spirit to help us. We have come to tell him how dreary the world now seems to us. Since he went away no flowers have bloomed. Our children have never seen the earth or the trees grow bright with their colours. We thank him for the sweet sap that we eat in place of the honey that the bees can no longer make, but we and our children long for flowers.'

'You have done well to come,' said the voice.

Then all at once the men were lifted up and, when they were set down again, they found that they were in the place where the Great Spirit had his Sky-Camp. Here the ground and all the trees were bright with never-fading flowers and the air was cool and full of scent. So bright were the flowers that it was as if many rainbows had been laid on the grass and across the tall bush.

When they saw this, the men stood and wept for joy and it was as if they were young again. Then the voice spoke once more.

'Gather as many of these flowers as you can hold in

your arms. Gather of every sort. When you have done this you shall be lifted back to the top of the mountain and from there you must go back quickly to your tribes.'

So the men obeyed. They spread out, and each gathered as many flowers as his arms would hold and, as soon as they had done this, they found that they were standing once more on the bare mountain-top. Again the voice spoke.

'Tell your tribes, when you take them these never-fading flowers, that they are the token of a promise. The earth shall never again be bare and dreary. All through the seasons a few flowers will always be sent to you by each of the different winds. But especially when the sweet-breathed east wind blows flowers shall grow among the grasses and on the trees as thick as the hairs on the skin of an opossum. With the flowers the bees will come back to you. Now make haste.'

So the wise men, carrying the flowers, began to hurry down the steep stone ladder, but this time the way seemed easy. Over the wide plains they went once more, over the stony ridges, and at last they were in the camp of their people.

Then all the men and women flocked round them and the children stared and all wondered at the beauty of the flowers and the delicious scent that filled the air.

The men told the tribes of the promise and, when they had all gazed long at the flowers, the men who had made the great journey stood up and scattered them far and wide. Some of these flowers fell on the tree-tops, some on the grassy plains, some on the bare stony ridges. Wherever they fell, flowers of their kind have always grown in such places ever since that day.

But in Australia the flowers grow most of all when the

sweet-breathed east winds come. Then they and the cool grasses shoot up, and once again it seems as if rainbows have been laid on the ground, and the trees and shrubs are so bright that it seems that their flowers are as many as the hairs on the skin of the soft-furred opossum.

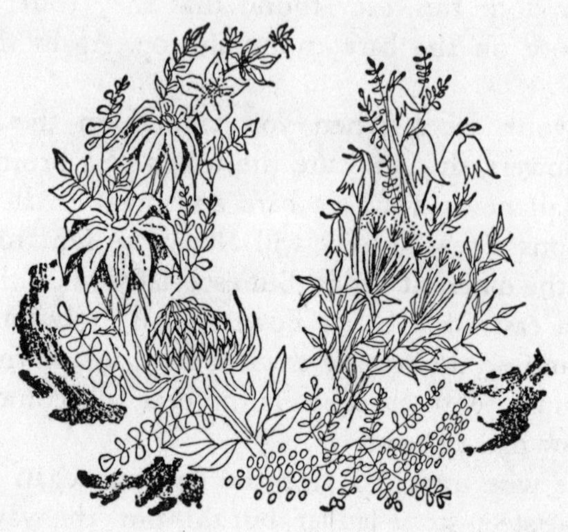

Biggoon & The Little Duck

Once upon a time, far away in a lonely part of Australia, there was a pretty young duck who liked to play about all by herself in the creek, but the older ducks in her tribe and the old drakes used to tell her that she shouldn't do that because there was a water-devil that lived further up the creek called Mulloka, and he'd catch her some day if she went so far away. But all she did was flap her wings, say she'd be careful and go on just the same.

One day, after she had swum quite a long way, she landed on a bank and there she saw some nice green grasses. She began feeding about when suddenly, out from a hidden place, rushed an enormous water-rat who seized hold of her.

The little duck struggled and struggled, but it was no good.

'I'm called Biggoon,' said the enormous water-rat. 'I live alone. I want a wife.'

'Quack, quack,' said the duck. 'Let me go. I'm not for you. I shall soon have a husband waiting in my own tribe. I don't belong to your tribe.'

'You just stay quietly with me,' said Biggoon, the great rat. 'I'm lonely here, and if you struggle or try to get away,

I shall knock you on the head, or else spear you with these spears,' and then the water-rat showed her the long sharp claws on his hind feet.

'Quack, quack! But if you hurt me my tribe will come and attack you,' said the duck.

'Oh no they won't,' said Biggoon. 'They'll think that the water-spirit, Mulloka, has got you. But even if they do come, let them, I'm ready,' and again he showed her the sharp claws on his hind feet.

So there was nothing for it, the duck had to stay. She was frightened of trying to escape while Biggoon the great rat watched her, so she pretended that she liked her new life and would stay with him, but all the time she was really thinking how she could get away. She knew that the ducks and drakes from her tribe came to look for her for she heard them. They were a kind of duck that make nests in trees, or on the ground, just as they please, so when they came to search for her they flew about and ran under all the bushes, but still they couldn't find her, because Biggoon had got her down in his big rat-hole. He kept her there all day because he knew that the people of her tribe would never come in the night because they were too much afraid of the water-spirit, Mulloka.

For a long while the little duck went on pretending to be quite contented, and at last the great rat thought that she really had settled down and would stay with him. So he gradually gave up watching her, and took his long sleep by day as he always used to, and went out at night as usual. HE wasn't in the least afraid of Mulloka the water-spirit. Then one day about noon, when Biggoon was particularly sound asleep, her chance came. She wriggled up out of the rat-hole and slid silently into the water. She swam away down the creek as quickly as she could towards her old camp. Suddenly she heard a sound behind her and she thought it must be Biggoon or perhaps even worse—Mulloka, the water-spirit. Of course, her wings were stiff by now because she had been living in a rat-hole all that time. However, she gave a great flap and managed to get into the air and she flew the rest of the way, alighting at last, very tired, among the ducks and drakes of her own tribe.

'Quack, quack, quack, quack!' They all gabbled round her at once, all asking questions and hardly giving her time to answer them. When they heard where she'd been, the mother ducks warned all the little ones only to swim downstream in the future because Biggoon would surely have vowed vengeance against them all now, so they mustn't risk meeting him.

The duck who had been a prisoner for so long was now very happy, what with being free and with her own tribe again. She splashed about all day in the creek and flew about at night if she wanted to. She roosted on the trees or she roosted on the ground, just as she pleased. But really she didn't roost much after being shut up for weeks.

It wasn't long before the laying season came and the ducks chose their nesting-place. Some decided on hollow trees, some preferred to go under bushes. When they had chosen, they all made nests, lined them with feathers and laid their eggs. After that the ducks sat patiently on the eggs, till at last little fluffy ducklings hatched out. Well, their mothers made them stay in the nests for a while, and then came the time when the ducks who had nested in the trees each took one of their ducklings on their backs and flew, splash, into the water with them, one at a time till they had got them all down. At the same time the ducks who had chosen to nest under the bushes all waddled out with their young ones after them.

In due time the little duck who had been imprisoned by Biggoon also hatched out her young ones. Her friends came swimming round the bush under which she had nested and said:

'Come along! Bring out your young ones. You must teach them to love the water as we do.'

Well, presently out she came.

Now all the other ducks had got five, six, seven, even eight children, but she had only two. What were they like? When they came walking out from under the bush after her, the other ducks all set up such a quacking as you never heard.

'What are those?' they shrieked out.

'Those are my children,' said the little duck proudly. She wouldn't let the others see that she herself was rather puzzled. The fact was that her children were quite different from all the other children of the tribe. Instead of being covered with downy fluff, they had soft fur; instead of two feet they had four. True, their bills were like ducks' and their feet were webbed, like duck's feet, but on their hind feet, just showing because they were still only just hatched, there were the points of little spears, claws that might some day be rather like Biggoon's.

'Quack, quack, quack! Take them away,' cried the ducks, flapping their wings and making a great splash. 'Take them away, they're more like Biggoon than us. Look at their hind feet—you can see the points of spears sticking out from them already! Take them away, or we shall kill them before they can grow up and kill us. They don't belong to our tribe, take them away! They've got no right here.'

Well, the other ducks made such a noise that the poor little duck went off with her two despised children of whom she had been so proud. She didn't know where to go. If she went up the creek Biggoon might catch her again and make her live in his rat-hole. He might kill the children, because they had webbed feet and bills and had been hatched out of eggs. He was sure to say, just as the ducks had, that they didn't belong to his tribe. It seemed that there would never be anyone but her to love her two unfortunate little ones, so she decided that she would take them right away. She began to swim up a side creek.

On and on she took them. The creek grew narrow and the mountains seemed quite near. But now she was far from anyone who knew her, far from Biggoon and her own tribe in a very secret place. So there she lived until her children were grown up.

As for the children, they seemed quite happy, and

when they laid eggs in their turn, the children that hatched out of those eggs were just like themselves.

To this day a few little people just like them can be found hidden away in Australia near mountain creeks. Now and then someone catches sight of one. If it is a tribesman he says:

'I have seen a gayardaree.'

If it is a white man he says:

'Would you believe it, I saw a duck-billed platypus?'

But whatever it is called, everyone quite agrees that this creature isn't like anybody else. When did a rat ever lay eggs? Or when did a duck have four feet?

Learning Magic

Once long ago, in China it was, there lived an idle fellow named Lee, who could read and write but was not at all fond of hard work. He thought indeed that it would be much pleasanter not to have to do any work at all, but to be a magician and earn a living in that way.

So off he went to a certain temple among the mountains and there he found the man he was looking for. This was an old priest, with crinkled-up eyes and a long beard, and Lee found him sitting very peacefully on a rush mat.

Making a low bow, Lee asked the priest if he would be kind enough to teach him magic.

'I am afraid you are not strong enough for that!' answered the old priest, shaking his head.

However, as the priest did not actually drive him away, Lee begged to be allowed to try: so at last the priest agreed to let him stay in the temple, with all the other pupils.

Early next morning the old priest sent for him, and, giving him a hatchet, told him to go out and cut firewood. Well, Lee did this, though it wasn't at all his idea of learning magic. However, next day it was the same; he kept being sent to do wood-cutting and went on doing it every day for a month, until his hands were so sore from chopping and his feet were so sore from carrying logs, that he began to wish himself home again.

One evening, when he came back from the wood, tired out as usual, he found two strangers drinking wine with the priest.

It was getting rather dark, but no candles had been brought in. However, instead of sending one of the pupils for a light, the old priest took a pair of scissors, cut a round out of a piece of paper, and then stuck the round of paper on the wall. Immediately it became as bright as the moon, and softly lighted the whole room.

Then it was the turn of one of the strangers. He took out a pretty, but rather small wine-flask, and told all the pupils to help themselves. Lee wondered how they were all going to get enough to drink out of such a small flask, but, to his astonishment, there was plenty for everybody and very good wine too.

'Why not,' said the second stranger, 'ask the Lady of the Moon to come and join us?'

The old priest agreed that to do this would be delightful, so this second stranger picked up a chopstick and threw it into the paper moon that was lighting everything so nicely. Then, at once, a lovely and beautifully dressed girl stepped out. At first she was only about a foot high—just about as big as that chopstick, in fact. But, on reaching the ground, she became as tall as an ordinary girl. She had a voice like a flute and sang a pretty song; when she had finished singing, she danced one dance after another. At last she jumped up on the table, where, to the astonishment of the pupils she became a chopstick again.

'This has all been very pleasant,' said the first visitor to the old priest, as the strangers rose to go, 'but now we must bid you good-night. We have planned to drink a glass of wine in the palace of the moon.'

The strangers then picked up their magic wine-flask and walked into the paper moon which still hung on the wall, and, after that, they could be seen in it quite plainly, talking

and drinking together. By and by this paper moon suddenly went out. One of the pupils brought in candles and they all saw that the priest seemed to have been sitting in the dark quite alone, except for the pupils. All the same, the round of paper was still there on the wall.

The priest didn't say anything at all to explain all this, but just told the pupils that they had all better go to bed, so that they should not be late with their wood-cutting in the morning.

Soon after, when nothing exciting seemed likely to happen again, Lee felt that he could not stand all this wood-chopping any longer, and, as the old priest seemed not to have any idea of teaching him any magical tricks, he went to him and said:

'Venerable Sir! I have been here in your temple for three months, doing nothing except chop firewood, which is a kind of work to which I was never accustomed before. I now wish to go home.'

'Certainly! That's all right!' said the priest. 'I told you that you were not strong enough. You can go home tomorrow if you like.'

'Honoured Sir,' said Lee, 'I have worked quite hard for you all this time. Please do condescend to teach me at least one little trick.'

'Why not?' said the priest. 'What sort of trick would you like to learn?'

'Well,' answered Lee, 'I have noticed that whenever you walk about anywhere, you are not stopped by walls; you just walk through them. Teach me how to do this, and I shall be satisfied.'

The priest laughed and told him some words in Chinese and, as the priest said them, he walked through the wall of the room and back again.

Lee managed to repeat the words, and, as he said them, he walked up to the wall, but found that he couldn't get through it as the old priest had done.

'Don't go so slowly!' said the priest. 'Put your head down and run at it.'

Lee, still repeating the words, did as he was told.

It worked! The next moment he found himself outside the temple. Delighted at this, he went back in the ordinary way to thank the priest.

'Be very careful not to show off too much,' said the priest.

'You'll be tempted to do just that, but I warn you! You'd better not.'

Sure enough, when Lee got home he went about bragging of having learned a great deal of magic while he had been up at the temple, but he was careful not to say exactly what he could do. Naturally enough, people didn't believe his story.

So, at last, he decided to show them. Then, saying the words, he put his head down and ran at the nearest wall. But he only hit the bricks so hard that the force of it knocked him down flat on the ground. When he was picked up poor Lee had a bump on his forehead as big as an egg and the story of Lee and his wall kept people laughing for a very long time.

The Story of Silly Cham-ba

—1—

THE SILLIEST BOY in Tibet in the old days was a boy called Cham-ba. But listen to what happened to him and then, if anyone ever calls you silly, you'll feel better about it. Yes, you really will, in spite of one or two things that happened to Cham-ba on the way to the good luck that came to him in the end, and besides I'm quite sure that nothing that you've ever done was half as silly as the things that he did.

The village in which Cham-ba lived with his poor old mother lay on the slopes of a huge mountain, and I'm sorry to say that the other boys of that village enjoyed teasing Cham-ba. It was fun, because he was so silly that he would believe almost anything that he was told.

One day Cham-ba went for a walk in one of the flowery valleys that lie among the high mountains of Tibet.

Because it was summer and because the sun had been shining for a week down by the river, all the flowers you can think of were in full bloom—blue, white, purple, and especially yellow flowers. All these kinds grew among the grasses. Cham-ba knelt down to smell some of them, when a young man passed by on the path.

'Hullo, Cham-ba!' he shouted. 'The soles of your feet are yellow!'

Cham-ba turned his head and looked at the soles of his bare feet. They certainly were rather yellow (it was really the yellow pollen from all those flowers).

'Yes, they are a bit yellow!' agreed Cham-ba. 'But what's wrong with that?'

'Oh, don't you know?' said the young fellow, trying not to laugh. 'Having yellow soles to your feet means you are going to die!—not some time, but now. At once!' And with that the teasing young fellow strode off down the path, taking care not to laugh till he was out of earshot.

But Cham-ba, who usually believed what he was told, believed this nonsense about yellow soles. He wasn't exactly frightened, he just sat down and thought. He thought about something that he'd noticed, and what he'd noticed was this, that, in the village, when someone died, a grave was always dug for them.

'So it stands to reason that I shall need a grave too!' he said to himself.

Now it happened that someone had left an old half-broken spade at the side of the path, so Cham-ba took it and, going down towards the stream which ran not far off down the flowery valley, he found a nice soft stretch of sandy gravel and then, with the half-broken spade, he dug himself a grave. He dug for a while and still it wasn't a very deep grave, but as he was tired of digging he thought it would do nicely. So down he lay in this shallow grave. Then he folded his hands and shut his eyes and kept quite still.

It wasn't long before a man came down the path. He was one of the King's servants and had been sent from the palace for oil; he was carrying it in a big earthen jar that fitted a wicker frame on his back. When he came near to where Cham-ba was lying, he happened to sit down to rest for a minute and began to look about him. As you can guess, he was rather surprised when he saw a boy lying on the riverside where the path came near the water. So he spoke to Cham-ba.

'What's the matter with you?' says he.

'The soles of my feet are turning yellow, kind sir, and that's a sure sign that I'm going to die,' answered Cham-ba. 'So I thought it was best to make myself a grave. As you can see I'm just lying in it and waiting.'

'What nonsense!' answered the servant. 'You couldn't talk like that if you were really dying! Get up at once and help me carry this jar of oil to the King's palace. Then for a reward, I'll give you a hen.'

'A hen? A live hen? All for myself?' asked Cham-ba.

'Yes, of course, all for yourself!'

Cham-ba thought it would be splendid to have a hen of his own, and as he settled the wicker contraption which held the jar of oil on his back and began to walk along by the King's servant, he began planning what he would do. The hen would lay dozens of eggs and of course all the eggs would hatch out and all the chickens would grow and then, thought Cham-ba, he'd be able to sell the cockerels and pullets, and buy a cow and sell milk and so on. Then he went on to decide the sort of wife he would marry, the nice house they would have, and, most important of all, how he would bring up the child they were sure to have.

'I shall bring him up most carefully!' decided Cham-ba, 'and be very kind to him when he's good. But what if he's naughty? I shan't beat him of course, but I shall make quite sure he understands that he must do as he is told. I shall just stamp my foot to show I'm in earnest! And with that Cham-ba really did stamp his foot there on the path. He stamped it so hard that the oil jar slipped in the wicker contraption and almost all the oil was spilled.

You can guess how angry the servant was.

'Stupid, clumsy, careless fellow! Idiot! Why did you stamp your silly great foot like that? Now look what you've done!'

Well, of course, when poor Cham-ba tried to explain why he had stamped, the man got crosser than ever and wouldn't listen. The end of it was that, as soon as they got to the palace, Cham-ba was dragged before the King. The man held him by one ear.

'We were walking quite quietly along the path, your Majesty,' said he, 'and suddenly this stupid fool of a boy began to stamp his foot—just at nothing! Like a madman! That's how your Majesty's oil came to be wasted!'

'Boy! Explain!' said the King. 'Why did you stamp your foot? Let go his ear and let him answer.'

So then poor Cham-ba fell on his knees and, for the second time, he tried to explain all about the hen, the eggs, the cow, the milk, the wife, the house and especially about how carefully he was going to bring up his little boy....

'So you see your Majesty ...' went on Cham-ba.

'Stop, stop!' said the King with tears of laughter streaming down his cheeks. 'That's the silliest story I've ever heard! I shall fall off this throne if you go on! Go back to your mother, boy, and give her this!' and with that he signed to one of the attendants to give Cham-ba a golden coin.

—2—

Now, as you have heard, all Cham-ba's plans about the hen came to nothing, but over the gold coin that he got for amusing the King, his mother took a hand. She was very sensible and, by careful trading—by always buying things cheap and selling them dear, by such ways as that—she really did manage to make some money. She made enough to buy a horse and also good clothes for herself and for Cham-ba, and more than that, she managed to get the well-off parents of a certain girl to agree that the girl should marry Cham-ba.

The bride's parents lived some way off. They were people whom the mother had met when she was away trading, so they didn't know that, though he was so good-natured, Cham-ba was also very silly, or that everyone in his own village laughed at him.

Now in those days, in Tibet, when a young man married, he usually went to live for some time with his bride's parents and this was arranged for Cham-ba. So one day, a cheerful party of horsemen arrived from the bride's family to bring the bridegroom to his new home. Of course Cham-ba had to dress up in his best clothes and of course the party from the bride's family had to be given a feast.

Like that, it began to get rather late—but everyone was enjoying the feast and said that it didn't matter. The way over the mountains wasn't difficult and there would be a splendid full moon that night. When they had all finished eating, Cham-ba begged the others to start and to ride on ahead. He said he would catch them up as soon as he had said good-bye to his dear old mother. So they did and his mother cried a little and Cham-ba cried a little and then, at last, he mounted his horse and set out to ride after his bride's relations. By this time the moon was up and it wasn't very dark so he thought he could easily catch them up.

But, as he rode, Cham-ba caught sight of his own shadow travelling along beside him. He couldn't make out what the shadow was, but felt sure that it must be some ghost or demon which was after him, for the dreadful thing was that it kept imitating everything he did and so did its horse. The faster Cham-ba galloped the faster went his shadow! Then he thought he would try to frighten the thing, so he took off his hat and threw it at it as hard as he could. When that didn't make it run away, he threw his cloak and then, one thing after another, all his wedding clothes, everything he had on. But none of this helped, and still the shadow came after him, imitating everything he did and frightening him dreadfully.

So, in desperation, poor Cham-ba jumped off his horse, threw down the reins, and ran along the road on foot, until he got into the shade of some big poplar-trees growing near the path-side. Once he was under the trees he stopped to take breath, and noticed, to his great joy, that the dreadful thing that had kept on following, had disappeared.

But, oh dear, when he peeped out from behind one of the

tree-trunks, from whichever side he looked out, the shadow immediately peeped out too. What was he to do? It seemed to him that the safest place must be this clump of trees, so he climbed up into the branches and very soon fell fast asleep.

Some time later, when the night was almost over and dawn was just beginning, a party of travellers on horseback happened to be passing along that way, and, coming to the path along which Cham-ba had ridden, what was their surprise to find a lot of very good clothes—wedding clothes—thrown here and there along the way. Naturally they had picked the things up as they came to them, and, last of all,

they found Cham-ba's horse quietly grazing. They brought the horse along with them as well and, when they got to the place where the poplar-trees grew, they decided to stop. So they sat down on the ground to share out the things they had found.

'You can have the hat,' said one.

'These boots just fit me,' said another.

At that Cham-ba woke up, and looking down he called out:

'I say! I want my share too, you know!'

Now the travellers had not been quite easy in their minds about taking the things, and so, when they heard a

mysterious voice coming from the tree, they were frightened. Perhaps the clothes were a trap of some sort? Perhaps the voice was that of a demon who lived in the tree? So they at once jumped up, sprang on to their horses and made off as fast as they could, leaving Cham-ba's horse and all the clothes behind them. So then Cham-ba climbed down from the tree and put on his wedding clothes again, not at all afraid now because the shadow wasn't there any more in the dawn light. Mounting his horse, he rode off quite cheerfully to his bride's house.

When he got there, her parents hurried out to greet him, and after asking him why he hadn't got there sooner, told him that people had come to the wedding from far and near and then they quickly led him to the room where the wedding feast was laid out. Now the food at this feast was very good indeed. There was brick tea with yak's butter, there was also fine Chinese food such as crispy noodles and water chestnuts, pork in sweet sauce, there was a sheep roasted whole, partridges, little honey cakes, and white bread.

Cham-ba kept looking at the bride whom he had only seen once before. He thought she looked very grand in her wedding clothes, for her dress was made of heavy silk and its collar-clasp was made of gold. She wore a necklace of big turquoises, little embroidered boots, and a wide turquoise ring almost like a crown round her long thick hair which was arranged on the top of her head.

Cham-ba, who was very fond of his mother, kept wondering to himself how he could save something nice for her to eat, and he managed to get hold of a narrow-mouthed copper jug. This he hid in his lap, and then, whilst he was eating his food, he every now and then dropped into it something particularly nice which he thought his mother would enjoy. Presently, however, without thinking, he by mistake thrust his hand right into the jug, and then to his horror he found that he couldn't draw his hand out again. Soon the bride's parents noticed that he seemed to have stopped eating and kept pressing him to have a little more. Poor Cham-ba was still hungry, but he was obliged to refuse everything and to say that he had already eaten enough.

Towards evening, when the feast was over, the guests went away, and Cham-ba was left alone with his bride. She too had noticed that he had stopped eating half way through the feast and now she began asking him what was the matter.

At first Cham-ba was too shy to tell her what had happened, but just hid his hand in his long sleeve. But after a great deal of coaxing she got him to show her what was wrong, and how his right hand was stuck in the neck of the copper jug.

'Never mind,' said she. 'There is a big white stone lying at the foot of the stairs. You had better slip down in the dark. This copper is quite thin and, by banging the jug against the stone, I'm sure you'll be able to free yourself.'

So Cham-ba went quietly down, till he saw what he thought must be the white stone, lying near the foot of the stairs. Creeping up to it, he raised his arm and—Bang! He brought down the copper jug on it. This did free his hand, but, to his horror, from the stone there came a muffled groan, and, stooping down to look more closely, Cham-ba found that instead of hitting a stone, he had hit the grey head of his bride's father, who, overcome by the feasting, had fallen asleep at the foot of the stairs.

Poor Cham-ba. He now felt sure that he must have killed the old man, and was so terrified that he decided to run for it, and, opening the door, he rushed off into the night.

—3—

After running for quite a long way in the dark he found himself near a neighbouring farm where, as it happened, a large honeycomb had been left lying in the corner of an open barn. It was dark and Cham-ba, not knowing what it was, stumbled into the barn, lay down upon the honeycomb and, tired with all these adventures, fell fast asleep. He had frightening dreams, and so he kept rolling about, and, like that, soon smeared himself all over with honey. Later in the night he woke up feeling very cold, and, creeping from the open barn into a shed close by that was used as a wool store, well pleased, he burrowed down into the soft warm wool, fell asleep at once, and slept until the first light of morning. Then, when he woke up, he struggled to his feet, looked down at himself and saw that he was all white and woolly.

'Oh dear,' he said to himself, 'I must have died! And now, because of my dreadful sin in killing my poor father-in-law, I must have been born again as a sheep!'

Then he felt himself all over and it seemed to him that he really and truly was covered with wool.

Poor Cham-ba! He didn't like the idea of being a sheep, in fact he felt very sad about it, but he thought, after all, it was a fair punishment for the dreadful thing he had done, even though he had meant no harm.

'The only thing now,' thought Cham-ba, 'is just to bear being a sheep as patiently as I can; then perhaps I shall be born as a man again, next time, as a reward. If I must be a sheep, I'll be as good a sheep as I can!'

So, dropping down on all fours and bleating softly, Cham-ba went slowly out of the courtyard and joined a flock of sheep which was grazing out on the steep mountainside.

Now the shepherd of these particular sheep was an old man and hadn't got very good eyesight, so he didn't notice either that there was one sheep too many, or that there was anything strange about this extra one.

Cham-ba wandered miserably about all day with the flock. He tried as best he could to do everything that the sheep did. But all that bleating made his throat ache and he found that mouthfuls of grass were most difficult to swallow. However, when evening came, he went meekly with the rest into the fold where they all slept.

Now it so happened that, that very night, sheep-stealers came prowling round that farm. They soon found the sheep-fold and started feeling about for a good heavy sheep. Then, finding that Cham-ba seemed to be the heaviest of them all, they picked him up, and one of them hoisted him on his back. Like that they carried him along for some distance until they got to the banks of a small stream. Here they halted, and, laying him down on the ground, they began to get ready to cut his throat. This frightened poor Cham-ba so much that, forgetting he was supposed to be a sheep, he called out:

'*Please* don't kill me! Please, please don't kill me!'

When they heard the sheep talking, the robbers were so frightened that they ran off as fast as they could.

When they had gone, Cham-ba got up from where they had thrown him. He felt quite worn out by all he had gone through, especially by trying to be a sheep all day.

'I spoke to those robbers,' he said to himself. 'But sheep can't talk, so what is the truth about all this?'

In the end he decided that he wasn't a sheep after all, and, much relieved, he made up his mind to go on to his bride's house.

So then things took a turn for the better, for, when he got there, he found that his old father-in-law wasn't dead after all, and when he explained just how it had all happened and how dreadfully he had been punished by having to be a sheep and then nearly getting his throat cut, his bride quite forgave him and persuaded her parents to take him into the house.

—4—

Now Cham-ba was a nice fellow, even if he wasn't very clever, so for a year or two he lived very happily with his young wife. But after a while he thought that he too really ought to make a little money and he remembered how his mother had made it by trading. So he got together a good stock of merchandise, loaded it up on pack-ponies, and set off on the way to India, where he felt he sure could sell at a good profit.

On the way, he halted one evening at a big inn. The landlord seemed a pleasant fellow and made him quite comfortable. While they were talking together after supper, this smiling landlord began telling some very extraordinary stories. Even Cham-ba thought that some of the things he said had happened were rather too wonderful to be true, and at last he said straight out that he could not quite believe all these tales.

'I am only telling you the truth,' said the landlord with a sly look, 'and I can prove it by showing you something stranger than anything I've told you. I will bet you that when it gets dark, a paper lantern will be carried into the room by a cat instead of by a servant.'

Cham-ba laughed and shook his head.

'I bet you anything you like that this won't happen,' he said.

'Very good!' said the landlord. 'We'll have a bet! If the lantern isn't carried in by the cat I will hand you over my house, my inn and everything I possess: but if the cat does what I say it will, you will have to give me all your ponies, all your merchandise.'

So the bet was arranged. Cham-ba was to get the inn and everything in it if the cat didn't bring in the lantern: the landlord was to get everything that Cham-ba had got if the cat did.

Now you must know that the landlord had specially trained his cat to do this very trick. The servants would light a small Chinese lantern and the cat would carry it in her mouth every evening just at dusk. The landlord had got quite rich by making this bet with travellers who came to his inn. Over and over again he had got ponies, goods and money.

So now, sure enough, just at dusk a large white cat came into the room where they were sitting. She was holding a lighted Chinese lantern in her mouth. After this, of course, the unfortunate Cham-ba was obliged to hand over to the landlord everything that he had brought with him for trading in India, and the ponies as well. He was quite a long way from home and, being now without money or goods, he decided that, rather than starve or beg, he would stay on in the inn as a servant. He felt ashamed of having lost all his goods, so he didn't send word back to his wife to say what had happened. But by now, as she had got very fond of him, she was very much worried when he did not return.

'I feel sure,' she said to herself, 'that my poor Cham-ba has got into some trouble or other. If everything had been all right he would have surely sent word. Quite a lot of people lately have been coming back that way, so he would have been sure to let us know.'

The end of it was that Cham-ba's wife decided that she would set out herself to see what had become of him.

It was quite usual in Tibet for women to go off trading, and she decided that it would be best to start with a few pack-ponies laden with wool.

As there was only one way across the mountains and down to India she knew she must be on the right track.

Sure enough, after travelling for about a week she got to the very inn where Cham-ba was working as a servant. Catching sight of him, she hid for a while, and then crept out and spoke to him when he was outside doing some kind of work on his own.

You can well imagine how pleased Cham-ba was to see his wife again, especially when he had told her the whole story and when she didn't seem at all cross about his having made a bet about a cat.

'Don't say a word about me to anyone,' she told him after she had thought a little. 'I shall pretend not to know you at all, and I shall come to the inn as an ordinary traveller. But there is just one thing I want you to do for me, dear Cham-ba. Please catch three mice and keep them safely hidden in a little box where no one will hear them scratching or squeaking. Later on I will tell you exactly what you must do.'

So, when Cham-ba had disappeared into the inn again, along came his wife with her ponies and asked for a night's lodging.

Everything began as before. During the evening this smiling landlord got talking, and he told the same extraordinary stories that he had told her husband. Just as her husband had done, she said it was hard to believe all these things, and then of course the landlord said:

'I can prove that I am only telling you the truth by showing you something stranger still. When it gets dark, it is a cat and not a servant who will bring us a light.' Then he offered the same bet as he had offered Cham-ba.

'Well,' said she, 'I can scarcely believe it possible there has ever been a cat that will carry a lighted lantern. I should much have loved to have seen it, but I am so sleepy tonight I can't wait till it gets dark, or bother with bets, so let us talk about it in the morning.'

Next day, before it was time for breakfast, she slipped out of the inn on the excuse of seeing to her ponies, and, finding Cham-ba alone, asked him if he had got the mice.

Yes, he had, and he showed them to her in a little box which he had hidden inside his clothes. She had just had time to tell him exactly what to do with them, when the landlord called out that breakfast was ready and she had to hurry in again. The landlord had breakfast with her and when they had finished eating she said:

'I have thought a great deal about what you told me yesterday. I simply can't believe that you are right! So I'm ready to make a bet with you that a cat will *not* carry a lantern into this room when it is dusk.'

The landlord was delighted to hear her say this and made exactly the same bet that he had made with Cham-ba.

'If you are right, O Traveller,' said he, 'you get everything that I possess—my house and all my goods. If you are wrong, you will have to give me your ponies and your wool.'

'Done!' said she.

So that evening, when it was getting dark, they both waited together to see whether the cat would really appear, while Cham-ba hid himself in a corner outside. Just at dusk the servants lit the paper lantern and gave it to the cat, and she, carrying the lantern in her mouth, began to cross the courtyard towards the door of the room where the light was wanted. Then, when the cat was about half way across, Cham-ba let loose one of the mice. Out of the corner of her eye she saw it and was just thinking about rushing after it, when she remembered, and instead of chasing the mouse she walked on sedately towards the door. But then Cham-ba let go the second mouse, and the poor cat could hardly bear to let this one go too. This time she stood perfectly still, except that the end of her tail was twitching and her whiskers and the hair along her back were bristling, but all the same she mustered her strength and went dutifully on. Then, just as she had got to the door, Cham-ba let the third mouse out of his box, and this was too much for the cat.

Dropping the lantern she sprang across the courtyard, caught the mouse just as it was disappearing into a hole, and sat down and ate it.

Meanwhile, inside, Cham-ba's wife and the landlord were waiting, and it was getting darker and darker. Cham-ba's wife pretended to be angry.

'I told you it couldn't be done! You have lost your bet!' she said.

At last, very sadly, the landlord had to admit that he had. Then in came Cham-ba with a light and pretended to be very much surprised to see his wife.

In the end they didn't make the landlord give up his inn, only just the things that he had tricked out of travellers, including of course all that he had got from Cham-ba.

After this Cham-ba did not try to be a trader again, but went home with his wife and they all lived happy ever after.

The Country of the Mice

THERE WAS ONCE a part of Tibet where there were two strange laws. The first of these was that no one, on pain of death, might keep a cat. The second was that, in a certain valley—down which ran a big mountain stream—the monks of the nearby monastery must keep the stone embankment on their side in good repair. These two laws were made for a very special reason and if you read on you will know what that reason was.

The man who was, long ago, the King of this part of Tibet, was an excellent man. One day, as he was sitting on his throne in the inner courtyard of his palace, he was told that a very grandly dressed Mouse, with a number of attendant Mice, was at the gate, and that the Grand Mouse was asking to see him.

The King was very much amused at the idea of having a visit from a talking Mouse and he gave orders that this splendid fellow, and his attendants, were to be brought in at once.

Now it is the custom in Tibet for all visitors—at any rate on great occasions—to bring with them a present of a white silk scarf. When he came before the throne, the King was delighted to see that the Mouse knew all about this custom, and that he had brought, not exactly a scarf, but a beautiful single thread of white silk. This silk thread was handed by one of the Mouse attendants to one of the King's guards, with a low bow.

The King now politely bade the Mouse welcome and soon the visitor was explaining why he had come.

'O King,' began the Mouse, 'you must know that this year our harvest was bad, our crops have fallen short, and we are threatened with hunger and famine unless we can borrow enough grain to carry us through the winter; so I, who am ruler and chief of all the Mice of your country, stand before you here to ask you if you can help us. If you can lend us what barley and oats we need, we will not only pay you back faithfully at our next harvest, but, as interest, with more grain than you lend us.'

'Very well,' agreed the King. 'We will lend. How much do you want?'

'I think,' said the Mouse, 'that we shall need about one of your big barns full.'

'Good gracious!' said the King astonished. 'And if I really do lend you a whole barnful of grain, how in the world do you think you could ever carry it away?'

'Leave that to me!' replied the Mouse in a confident tone. 'If you will consent to lend us the grain, we will do the rest.'

So the King agreed to lend the Mice one of his great granaries full of barley and oats. He decided on the largest and ordered his officers to throw open its doors, and to let the Mice carry away as much as they wanted.

That night, the chief and ruler of the Mice summoned his subjects together, and, to the number of many hundreds of thousands, they came to the barn. Then each Mouse picked up as much grain as he could carry. One Mouse would hold it in his mouth, another in a tiny sack on his back, and others had some curious way of carrying it curled up in their tails. They made a very tidy job of it and when they had finished, the barn was completely empty, and not a single grain of oats or barley was left behind.

Next morning, when the King went out to look at his barn, he was very much astonished to find that the Mice really had been able to take the grain away so quickly, and he began to have a very high opinion of them.

'These are very efficient Mice,' said he to his courtiers.

When, after the next harvest, the chief and ruler of the Mice kept his promise and paid back the grain with interest, the King decided that the Mice were honest as well as clever.

Now it happened, not long after this, that the country over which this King ruled was attacked by the ruler of a neighbouring kingdom. This kingdom lay on the opposite side of the big mountain and river, and was far richer and more powerful than the country where the Mice lived. Soon a large army was on the march and ready to attack.

When the Mice heard what was happening, they were very much worried, for they feared that, if the enemy entered their country and dethroned the King who had been their friend over the loan of the grain, they themselves might not be so well off. In fact they did not like the idea of a strange ruler.

So the Mouse Chief put on his grandest robes, and, with his attendants, set out to visit the King again. When he got to the palace he again asked for an interview with His Majesty. He was shown in at once, and once more offered a single thread instead of the usual scarf. Finding that the King was looking very depressed, the Mouse Chief spoke at once in a grand but squeaky manner:

'I have come to you a second time, O King, in order to see whether I can be of use to you! The last time I was here you did me and my people a great favour, and if it is now in

our power to help in any way, we shall be very glad to do our best.'

In spite of feeling depressed about the war, the King could not but feel amused to hear such solemn words from a Mouse.

'I thank you very much,' said he, 'but really what could your excellent Mice do to help? We are threatened with invasion by a foreign army, outnumbering mine by many thousands. This army is already encamped just across the river. All the men I can muster will not be enough to prevent them from crossing as soon as they choose. Thank you yet again, but I don't see how Mice could help.'

'Do you remember, O King,' replied the Mouse in a calm

tone, 'that on the first occasion I was here you did not believe that we should be able to carry away the grain you had lent us, or to pay back the loan? And yet we proved ourselves able to do both! All we ask you now is to trust us again, and, if you will undertake to do one or two things which we shall ask of you, we, on our part, will undertake to rid you of the invading army.'

The King was very much interested and he replied:

'Very well, Mouse! What you say is true. I didn't believe last time you would be able to do what you said but I trusted you and I will trust you again. Tell me now what you wish my servants or my army to do, and I will see that they carry out our share of the bargain.'

'Very good,' answered the Mouse. 'All we wish you to do is to provide us, by tomorrow evening, with one hundred thousand sticks. Each stick must be about a foot long, and they must all be laid neatly in rows on the bank of the river. If you will undertake to do this, we on our side will undertake to put the opposing army in a state of confusion and panic! But I should like to add something more. If we succeed in doing all we promise, we shall, later, ask you to safeguard us against the two principal dangers which threaten our existence.'

'If you can really do what you say,' replied the King, 'I will certainly try to safeguard you against these dangers, if you tell me what they are.'

'The dangers to which I refer,' answered the Mouse, 'are, Gracious King, the dangers of Floods and Cats. Most of our mouse-holes—our homes—are in the low-lying land near the river, and whenever the snows melt and the river rises, it overflows this level country and floods our holes and nests. What we would suggest to Your Majesty, is that you should build a strong wall—an embankment—all along the river, so as to make sure that the water cannot overflow into our homes. As to Cats, they are always the persecutors of Mice, and we ask you to banish all Cats for ever from your Kingdom.'

'Very well,' replied the King 'if you can succeed in getting rid of the large and powerful army which now threatens us, I will undertake to do what you ask.'

On hearing this the Mouse Chief bowed low to the King, and, after making polite farewells, he went back as fast as he could to his own subjects.

Next morning, early, he sent out messengers to call together all the full-grown Mice of his kingdom, and, when they came, he gave them his orders. About dusk he was able to lead a large army, numbering several hundreds of thousands of Mice, to the bank of the river, where he found the sticks all neatly laid out exactly as the King had promised.

The Mice had fully understood the orders they had been given, and each small group at once proceeded to launch a stick on the river, by mean of which they soon crossed over to the other side.

It was quite dark by the time they got across and the enemy soldiers were all asleep in their camp. Some were lying in tents and some were lying outside in blankets, but all had their weapons beside them ready for any alarm. But no alarm was given. The Mice were soundless. They did not even need a word of command from their Chief, but at once scattered themselves through the camp, whereupon each one began to do as much damage as he possibly could in the shortest possible time.

Some went to the bowmen and nibbled their bow-strings: some went to where the musketeers were sleeping and gnawed through their musket-slings. Others bit holes in the clothes of the men and some bit off their pigtails. Others bit holes in sacks so that everything in them spilled.

In fact, these bold Mice attacked anything upon which their teeth could make an impression, so that tents, stores, grain, and provisions of all kinds were soon in shreds or scattered in confusion.

After a couple of hours of such silent work the Chief collected his Mouse army on the river bank, and, embarking on their stick-rafts once more, they paddled themselves quietly over to their own shore without a sound having been heard by the enemy.

But next morning, at day break, when the enemy soldiers began to stir, there was a fearful outcry in that camp.

Each man as he woke from sleep found himself in a woeful state—his clothes in rags, his pigtail nibbled, his bow-string gnawed, his musket without a sling to carry it or a fuse to light it. What was almost worse—there was nothing to eat for breakfast—No! Not a single crumb. Each soldier at once began to accuse the other of theft and treachery. Before many minutes had passed the whole camp was in an uproar, comrade quarrelling with comrade, and every man in the field was accusing the other.

The Mouse ruler had of course advised the King that now was the time for the King's small army to attack. He did not actually do more than march down to the river, but he flew the great flag in the blue sky and had the great drum beaten on the terrace of the palace. So, in the middle of their confusion, the enemy soldiers on the opposite bank saw the flag and heard the great drum and, terrified at the thought of having to fight in their present confusion, the whole enemy army took to flight.

As for the Mice, safe from Floods and Cats, they lived happily, and every year the King also provided for them a gift of grain in thankful recognition of the splendid help they had given him in time of need.

The King naturally wanted to make quite sure that there would not be any more invasions. What he did, after thanking the Mice, was to send a herald across the river to the enemy capital. The herald was told to say that, on this occasion, the King had only considered it worth while to employ a few Mice to defeat his enemies. But if he was ever threatened again, he would be ready to beat back the attack first with all his Cows, Sheep, Yaks, Cats and Dogs; and if they did not succeed, he would order out mountain Tigers, wild Dogs, Wolves and Bears, and if they failed, he would come out to war himself with all his warriors!

When the foreign ruler heard this message he was very

frightened and considered it wiser at once to make a Treaty of Peace.

'How,' he thought to himself, 'can I hope to defeat even the tame animals, let alone the wild beasts and the soldiers, of a country whose Mice can show such skill and courage?'

So peace was made and the two countries remained on friendly terms for many years after.

The Little Pet Rani

Once, long ago in India, there lived a Rajah. He not only reigned over a fine large kingdom but he was also a good man and had seven handsome sons. He treated them all well and all exactly alike. This was because he didn't want them to be jealous of one another. So to each of his seven sons he gave jewels, clothes made of embroidered brocade, and when they grew old enough, he had a splendid palace built for each of them. Each palace was a little different from the others, but no one could say which was the best or the largest.

At last the time came when all the seven sons were old enough to be married. But where was their father to find seven brides who would all be equal in every way? He wanted, you see, to find them seven maidens, each just as young, as lovely, and as clever, as one another—and as well each must be the daughter of good and high-caste parents.

The Rajah sent ambassadors all through his kingdom and to every neighbouring kingdom, but when they came back they said that though one maiden was lovely, and another played and sang most beautifully, and another was the daughter of high-caste parents, or of some powerful

King or Rajah, it seemed impossible to find seven maidens who were all equal in every way. What was to be done? The Rajah sent for his wise old Vizier.

'I cannot,' said the Rajah, 'and I will not, favour one of my sons and give him a better wife than the others. If I do, there will be jealousy between them. Their seven brides must be equal in every way.'

'Your ambassadors, great Rajah, have failed to find seven such maidens?'

'They have,' answered the Rajah.

The Vizier thought for a while. 'Highness,' he said at last, 'there is a proverb which says, "What man cannot accomplish should be left to Fate and chance".'

'But how is that to be done?' asked the Rajah. 'How can Fate and chance find seven maidens who are equal in every way?'

'Tell your sons, the seven Princes,' said the Vizier, 'to take their bows and arrows and climb to the top of the tallest tower in the city. Tell each of them to shoot off a marked arrow in any direction he chooses. Have watchmen posted to see where each of the marked arrows falls. The maiden who lives nearest to where his arrow falls shall be the bride of that Prince. Each Prince must, of course, promise that he will abide by the result.'

So the Rajah consulted his sons, and they agreed to this plan.

The best astrologers in the kingdom were asked to decide on the day when the stars and planets would be in lucky positions. All the many towers and minarets of the city were carefully measured to see which was the highest.

When the morning came for the trial, the seven Princes put on their most magnificent clothes, took their bows and arrows, and climbed up the tallest tower. Then, as soon as the sun had risen and the watchmen were posted, each

Prince drew his bow and shot his arrow.

They all felt anxious, for they did not know what sort of marriage chance would arrange for them, and each was afraid that he might have to marry someone too ugly or stupid to have found a husband already.

However, at first all went well, for six of the sons found, soon after they had shot their arrows, six beautiful and charming brides.

But the youngest son had shot his arrow farther than any of the others, and it had flown far and fast. Outside the city wall it flew, and disappeared into thick jungle. The watchmen had a long search, but at last they found it, stuck in one of the branches of a huge old banyan tree. Close to the arrow, and seeming to look at it with interest, a small monkey had perched herself. But there was no one else to be seen at all—certainly no maiden.

So they caught this little monkey and went back to the Rajah's court. They set her down before him as he sat on his splendid throne with the youngest Prince standing beside him. The watchmen salaamed and told their story.

'So Fate and chance do not mean me to have a bride,' said the youngest Prince, with a sigh.

'Of course you must have a bride, my son,' answered the Rajah. 'You must shoot again.'

'Father,' said the Prince, 'do not, I beg you, order me to break my word. I made a solemn vow, just as my brothers did, that I would do exactly as the luck of the arrow decided. It must be that Fate means me not to marry.' With that the Prince bowed to his father, picked up the little monkey and took her sadly home to his palace.

As it seemed that he was not to have a wife, he decided to make a pet of the little monkey. He put a diamond collar round her neck, fed her on delicious fruits, led her about on a golden chain and named her Rani, which means Queen. After a while he grew very fond of her, and the little creature soon seemed to love him in return.

Then came the time when the weddings of his six brothers were to be celebrated, and for each of them the Rajah made a great banquet.

But for the youngest prince there was no wedding feast, no joyful bringing home of the bride, no wedding portion. The Rajah, who loved all his sons, was sad at heart. Again he begged the youngest Prince to marry.

'Either shoot another arrow, my son, or else choose yourself a bride. I cannot bear to see you lonely and sad, when there is such joy over the weddings of your brothers.'

But nothing that his kind father could say would make the Prince break his vow, and the courtiers whispered among themselves that he must be mad.

After a few months the Rajah decided, as was the custom, to pay a visit to the palaces of his six married sons and his six beautiful daughters-in-law, and to give to each couple his blessing and yet more presents. In each of the six palaces there were great preparations and great joy. But in the seventh palace there was no beautiful daughter-in-law, there had been no wedding presents, and in fact nothing to rejoice about.

One evening when the last of these feasts was going on, and the whole sky was lit up by fireworks, the youngest prince sat alone in his garden. As she often did when he was sad, his little monkey climbed on to his knee and gently stroked his cheek with her paw.

'What shall I do, little Rani? I should like to entertain my father as my brothers have done, but how can I when I have had no marriage portion and haven't a wife to welcome him?'

What was his amazement when little Rani, the monkey, answered him. 'Do not be unhappy, dear master,' she said in a small, clear voice; 'invite your father, the Rajah, and all his court. Everything will be ready for them.'

The Prince stared at her, not believing his ears. He asked her many questions, but not another word did she say. Just as he began to believe that he must have fallen asleep and dreamed that she had spoken, she skipped off and, in a moment, came back. As she drew nearer he saw that she was carefully holding a little piece of broken china in her small paw. When she gave it to him he stared at her in bewilderment. Then looking carefully at the bit of china and turning it over, he saw that something was written on the back of it.

It was too dark to read the words, but taking it inside where a lamp had been lighted, he read what was written:

'TAKE THIS AND THROW IT INTO THE HOLLOW OF THE TREE FROM WHICH YOUR WATCHMEN FETCHED ME, AND BRING ME AN ANSWER.'

The bit of broken china was real enough and so were the words that were written on it. Again he begged the little monkey to speak to him, but never a word would she say.

Next day, very early, he sent for the watchmen who had found the arrow. Then, with them as his guides, he went out into the jungle. Sure enough, far in the jungle, there stood a huge old banyan tree. Its wide spreading branches had sent down roots and formed trunks of their own so that the old banyan was more like a grove than a single tree. In the middle of all these branches he came to the main trunk. It was so old that it had become hollow, and

the hollow was so big that he could have stood upright inside it. He did as he had been told and, into the great hollow trunk, he threw the little piece of broken china.

No sooner had he done so than a beautiful girl appeared in the opening. Beckoning to the Prince to come after her, she disappeared once more into the tree. He climbed in, but the beautiful girl had vanished, and the Prince found that he was in a dark twisting tunnel. Still he followed, and soon he was in daylight again. Not only was he in daylight, but the jungle had disappeared and he was in a beautiful garden. The trees had gold and silver fruits on them, and the little stream that ran among them flowed, not over pebbles, but over sparkling jewels. From a marble pool hundreds of fountains rose into the air. Beyond the pool and the fountains he could see a splendid terrace supported by twelve arches. He walked on. A flight of marble steps led to the terrace and there, on a jewelled throne, sat a maiden so beautiful that he fell in love with her at once.

'So you have come, Prince,' said she and smiled. 'Thus far it is good. But you must come no nearer. Go back to your palace and send a message to your father the Rajah, inviting him and his court to a feast. You need do nothing more. Look at this garden and set your mind at rest. Everything will be fit for a Prince and a great Rajah.'

So, since she forbade him to come any nearer to her, the Prince did as she told him and went home. When he got to his palace, Rani, his little monkey, was waiting for him. He told her everything that had happened, how he was to do nothing but send a message of invitation to his father, how the mysterious lady was the most beautiful he had ever seen, and how he had fallen deeply in love with her. But though the little monkey seemed to listen to everything, she said not a word—though, as you can guess, the Prince begged her to speak. Then, though he doubted what

might come of it, he sent the invitation to the Rajah and all his courtiers.

Next morning at daybreak he was awakened by a great stir in the palace. He looked out into the courtyard and saw that servants whom he had never seen before were bustling about. It seemed as though they were making preparations for a splendid feast.

Cooks were busy, other servants hurried about carrying great silver trays of delicious food, and there was the sound of music.

As soon as he went out into the garden he found new pools, terraces and fountains. The small gardens of his palace had been changed till they seemed as lovely as the magic one in which he had walked when he went through the trunk of the banyan-tree.

The Rajah and his courtiers, of course, knew nothing of all these changes, for the youngest son's palace was some way off and its garden had a high wall round it. Again the courtiers whispered, saying that this invitation must mean that the youngest Prince really had gone mad, for he surely had not enough treasure to invite the whole court. However, when the time came for the feast they all set off.

They found that not only had the garden changed and become far more beautiful, but the furniture of the palace was so splendid that they were amazed.

'Who can have done all this?' said his six brothers, who were there with their wives. 'It must have been his bride, and yet we did not even know that he was married.'

They all crowded round the Prince and asked him about this wonderful new sister-in-law, but the youngest Prince would say nothing. Indeed, he felt rather sad. He could see that all these changes were very splendid and he felt truly grateful to the little monkey for what she had done. 'But,'

thought he, 'what shall I say after the feast when, as is the custom, they ask to meet my bride and when all I can show them is a little monkey?' They all sat down to the feast, and when it was over, the youngest Prince went away to the room where he had left Rani.

What was his amazement to find there, not the little monkey, but the beautiful and mysterious lady whom he had last seen in the enchanted garden. This time she did not forbid him to come near. Instead, she came sweetly up to him.

'Prince,' said she, 'you wanted a bride. Here I am. As soon as I saw you, I fell in love with you, just as you did with me.'

The Prince kissed her tenderly, but then he looked round at the golden stand on which his little monkey usually liked to sit and saw that she was not there. He looked round the room—there was still no sign of her.

'What are you looking for?' said the mysterious lady.

'My little pet monkey isn't here,' said the Prince, 'and it is to her that I owe everything. What can have become of her?'

'Does a monkey matter to you when I am here?' asked the lady, frowning a little.

'This monkey will always matter to me,' said the Prince.

'But it was I,' she said, 'not the monkey who did all this for you. Are you ungrateful?'

'No indeed,' said the Prince. 'I thank you, beautiful lady. I love you and I will be your slave for the rest of my life. But I want my poor little monkey, and I'm afraid that some harm may have come to her.'

'You will never see her again,' said the lady, but this time she smiled as she spoke. 'Don't grieve! *I* was that monkey. When your arrow quivered in a branch of my banyan-tree, I changed myself into a little monkey because I wanted to

test you, and to see if you would keep your vow. You have been faithful to it and have even been faithful to your poor monkey, even now, when I myself told you to forget her.'

Once more the Prince gazed at the beautiful lady in amazement.

'It was I,' she went on, 'whom you brought home to this palace, I who wore the diamond collar and the golden chain, I who comforted you when you were sad, I who spoke to you in a human voice. If you don't believe me, look, here is the monkey skin.'

Then the Prince saw that this must be the truth, and embraced her joyfully. Soon he brought in his good old father, the Rajah, and his six brothers and sisters-in-law, who were all delighted with his lovely bride.

And the youngest Prince and his beautiful Rani lived happy ever after.

Mr. Korbes the Fox

Once upon a time, not in your time nor in my time, but in a very good time, Cockie Lockie and Henny Penny decided to go on a journey together. Some say one thing and some another about why they wanted to travel. What is certain, however, is that they thought they would first call on Mr. Korbes the fox. This was because he had invited them both to dinner. The cock had a beautiful carriage with four red wheels—and to this carriage he harnessed four sleek, well-trained mice.

When everything was ready, the cock and the hen sat down in the carriage and the cock called out:

'Now mice be ready
And wheels run steady
For we're all on our way
A visit to pay
To Mr. Korbes the fox today.'

Then the mice at once set off at a good pace.

After a while they met a cat and stopped the carriage to talk to her.

'Where are you going?' says she.

'First to the house of Mr. Korbes,' answered the cock.

'Take me with you,' says the cat.

'Certainly,' says Cockie Lockie. 'But take care you don't dirty my beautiful red wheels as you get in.' Then he started the carriage again.

'Now mice be ready
And wheels run steady
For we're all on our way
A visit to pay
To Mr. Korbes the fox today.'

They went and they went, and they kept meeting people on the way who all wanted to know where they were going. When they heard, they all wanted to come too. So the mice and the carriage with the beautiful red wheels stopped again and again, first for a needle then for a pin, and then for a duck, who all got into the carriage drawn by the four mice. Each time when he wanted to start off again, Cockie Lockie said the same thing:

'Now mice be ready
And wheels run steady
For we're all on our way
A visit to pay
To Mr. Korbes the fox today.

Last of all they met a millstone. Luckily, they were quite near Mr. Korbes's house by this time, because as you can guess the millstone was rather heavy. However, in he got, and for the short way that was left the mice managed quite well.

When they got to the house, Cockie Lockie and Henny Penny both got down out of the carriage and went to ring the door-bell.

While they were doing this the others began to talk among themselves and what they all said was that it was not really at all safe for a cock and a hen to go and visit a fox. The duck especially quacked a great deal, saying how dangerous she thought it always was to visit such a person.

Next moment, Cockie Lockie and Henny Penny came back. Mr. Korbes seemed to be out, they said, and they had decided to wait for him. The others nodded to each other and the cat spoke:

'Cockie Lockie and Henny Penny, we all thank you very much for bringing us here in your beautiful carriage with the red wheels. But we think that, as Mr. Korbes is a fox, he is not really the right kind of friend for you.'

The duck quacked to show how much she agreed with what the cat was saying.

'Why not?' said Cockie Lockie in surprise. 'He specially invited us to come to dinner with him as soon as our beautiful carriage with the red wheels was ready.'

'I dare say he did,' answered the cat, 'But we think that the wicked sly-boots invited you simply because he meant to eat you both.'

When she heard that, Henny Penny was so frightened that she fainted and Cockie Lockie looked round him in terror, wondering how they could possibly escape. But the others had thought of a better plan than trying to escape.

First, the mice drew the carriage into the barn. Then the others unharnessed them and the mice hid. The next thing was for the others to creep quietly into the empty house and to take up their positions ready for Mr. Korbes.

After a while, home he came. He soon noticed with

pleasure that there was a smell just like the smell of a hen-house or a duck-house. You may not think that this a very delicious kind of smell, but Mr. Korbes liked it very much and what's more, he thought that this smell might have something to do with his sly plan of inviting a cock and a hen to dinner. Perhaps they had been here and just gone for a walk and would soon come back. So he thought to himself that there would be no harm in having a nice fire ready to cook them. So he fetched in some more wood and he bent down to blow a bit of flame into the dead-looking ashes on his hearth.

But good gracious, what was that? He heard a terrible angry screech and then a cloud of ashes spurted up into his face so that he was nearly blinded. (That was the cat.) He couldn't see properly, so he went to wash his face in a pail of water that he always kept ready in the scullery. But as soon as he tried to wash, all the water in the pail seemed to splash up and in a moment he was wet through. (That was the duck.) He went to where his towel hung and had hardly begun to dry his face when he felt two dreadful long scratches, one on each cheek. (That was the pin and the needle who had both hidden in the towel.) Mr. Korbes began to dance about with rage, and as he rushed to the door cried out in a fury:

'The house is bewitched! The house is bewitched!'

But the millstone had managed to balance itself on the top of the lintel and as Mr. Korbes rushed out, down it fell, thump on the top of him. And that was the end of Mr. Korbes.

Now all this time Cockie Lockie and Henny Penny had been sitting perched up on a high beam and when they were quite sure that now the fox could do them no harm, they came fluttering down. They had of course seen everything that happened and now they thanked the others most heartily for all they had done.

They all decided that Mr. Korbes's house was one of the nicest they had ever seen, so the end of it was that they settled down in it, and all lived happily there together for the rest of their lives. Cockie Lockie often harnessed up his mice, and took the others for drives in his beautiful carriage with the red wheels.

How Urseli Became a Princess

—1—

IN A BEAUTIFUL VALLEY up among many high mountains—in Austria it was—there once lived a rich old farmer who had three daughters. The neighbours didn't like the family very much and used to call the girls by nicknames: 'Proud Katel', 'Lazy Gretel' and 'Foolish Urseli'. When you get to the end of the story, you can decide whether or not you think these nicknames were fair.

But there is one thing you must know about at once. It was the custom—and still is—in the farms that lie in the valleys between those big snow mountains (the Alps they are) to drive the cows up for the summer to the high pastures. The farmers do this because, high up, there are the very best meadows, and in these high meadows, directly the winter snow has melted, the sweetest and freshest grass will sprout. Up there too grow the best flowers of all, high up, among the short turf and grey rocks.

One summer day, about a fortnight after this particular rich farmer had driven his herd of cows up to one of these high summer grazing-places, the dairymaid (who had stayed up there to look after them) came running down, all out of breath, and looking for all the world as though a bear were after her. She had of course been living in the pretty little hut that was next to the dairy, milking the cows and making the butter and cheese. There she ought still to have been, but not at all! Here she was, back at the farm, panting after her run down the mountain, looking as white as a tablecloth, and telling everyone that all the cows had disappeared.

'Nonsense, girl!' said the farmer. 'They can't have gone! Alpen Rose, now, she has a great big bell, so how could she have disappeared? Then the white one, Schnee Glockchen, she has got such a good bell that you can hear it as far as you can hear an alpenhorn! All the cows have got good bells! You just didn't listen out for the beasts, my girl! You just came running down without thinking! Now just you go back up again, and listen out for them.'

But no! The girl simply wouldn't go back up! She wouldn't go back to her nice little hut and her dairy, not for anything! She cried and she hollered and she declared that the place was haunted! She sobbed and she said that the farmer was a brute to ask her to go! The place was haunted and that was sure! She was going back to her mother.

The farmer said he wouldn't listen to such nonsense, he called her a silly feather-head, said it was all a fuss about nothing! And at last, when she still wouldn't go and set off back to her mother, he shouted for his eldest daughter:

'Katel, Katel!' he shouted. 'Just pack yourself a bit of food and go up to the summer pasture! That silly idiot of a dairy-girl says she's lost the cows!'

Well, Katel didn't want to go. She wasn't called Proud Katel for nothing, and to go up and see to the cows wasn't at all the kind of work she cared to do. However, she knew her father wasn't the sort to stand any nonsense so, with a very sulky look on her face, she began to get ready. First she packed herself some food, all of the best ham, butter, eggs, white bread, cake and a bottle of wine as well. Then she changed her shoes and, at last, she started off up the path with her nose in the air and looking as if the ground wasn't good enough for her feet.

When she got to the summer pasture there was the hut all right. The girl had left the door open and Katel could see that there was no one inside and that the fire had gone out.

The cow-byre was empty too and so was the dairy. When she listened she couldn't hear any cow-bells. In fact, there wasn't a sound up there except for the light summer wind among the rocks.

'Drat the stupid cows!' Katel said to herself crossly. However, she looked about and thought she'd see where the newest-looking marks of cows' hoofs led. The marks led across the grassy slope and went on towards a sort of dark hollow.

She went to have a better look and when she got nearer, though she couldn't exactly see, she felt sure that she could hear something in the hollow. It wasn't a cow-bell though, nor yet was it mooing. What it sounded like was a human voice, calling out for help. The hollow was rocky and steep, narrow too, and rather slippery from the splashing of a little waterfall. However, Katel went carefully to the edge, rather afraid of slipping, and there, down on the bottom, she saw an ugly little old man with white hair and a white beard. He was trying to climb out and crying:

'Lend me a hand, lend me a hand, young lady! You're young and strong! I'm old and weak!'

Katel looked at him, but she could see that if she went down she would get her pretty white stockings and her embroidered petticoats wet. So she just pretended not to hear and went back to the hut. But the funny part of it was that she never got there.

— 2 —

Down in the valley at home her father got on with the usual farm work. He quite expected that Katel might spend the night up at the hut, but next day, not long before dinner-time, he began to wonder what had become of her.

'Gretel!' he called to his second daughter. As there was no answer he guessed where she was and off he went to the hay-barn. There she was, curled up in the warm hay and fast asleep.

'Get up, you lazy thing!' he said, and, when he had given her a poke, she did, at last, sit up and rub her eyes. 'Your sister Katel hasn't come back from the summer pasture,' he told her. 'She went up yesterday to the dairy to look for the cattle that that silly fool of a dairymaid said were lost. Just pop up and see what has become of her.'

Well, Gretel didn't a bit want to walk up all that way. She yawned and stretched and pulled bits of hay out of her hair. However, at last she slipped down out of the hay, went into the kitchen and she too packed a big basket of food. As she walked the steep path up to the summer pasture, she often sat down for a rest, and ate tasty bits out of her basket while she was getting her breath.

Just the same things happened to her as to her sister. The hut door was open, the cow-byre was empty—and so was the dairy. She found the hoof-marks, followed them to the dark hollow, and saw the same little man scrabbling about down there, and calling pitifully for help. But Gretel wouldn't help him out any more than Katel. It wasn't her pretty clothes she was bothered about, but, as she shouted down to him, it would be too much trouble to scramble down and then to get out again. So off Gretel started for the hut and she never got there either.

— 3 —

That night there was only one daughter left in the farm—that was the one they called Foolish Urseli.

'Father,' said she next morning, after she had given the farmer his breakfast, 'Katel hasn't come back and now Gretel hasn't come back. The dairymaid has said she won't go up and nobody knows where the cows are. Nobody knows whether the poor things have even been milked. Don't you think I'd better go up and see?'

'*You* go!' cried her father. 'What makes you think *you* could manage anything when your two clever sisters couldn't?'

'You never know!' said Urseli.

'That's true enough!' said he. 'Go if you want to.'

Well, it was just like Foolish Urseli not to pack herself a proper dinner. She left her father a good meal, it's true, but for herself she only took a few bits of rindy cheese and the stale heel of a loaf of bread.

On the way up she didn't trip along proudly like Katel, and Gretel, she just tramped along singing, so it wasn't long before she got to the summer dairy.

There was the door of the hut, still open, but there was no one inside and no trace anywhere of her sisters, nor could she see the cows and, when she listened, all she could hear was the wind in the rocks. This time the wind was stronger, in fact it was moaning a bit, and some big clouds were forming among the mountain-tops.

'The weather's going to change,' thought Urseli, nodding to herself.

Anyhow it wasn't raining yet, so the hoofprints of the cows were still plain and she followed them just as her sisters had done, and so she too was led to the dark hollow. Just like them she thought she could hear someone calling as she got nearer, and when she was near enough to look down, there was the little old man, still scrabbling about and calling for help.

'Lend me a hand! Lend me a hand, young lady! You are young and strong! I am old and weak!'

Well, Urseli never thought twice.

'You silly old thing!' said she. 'However did you get down into such a place?' She rolled up her sleeves and down she went, ready to pull the poor little old man up.

'Which side of the hollow do you want to go?' she asked when she got to him.

'This way,' he said in weak voice, and instead of pointing up he pointed to a narrow passage between the rocks which led to a little broken-down house that Urseli had not noticed before.

Just as they got to the house, there was a tremendous clap of thunder and one of those big summer storms came on, the sort they have among those kind of mountains. Soon the thunder was fairly rolling round and the wind was roaring, the rain was coming down in torrents, the lightning seemed to be crackling, but Urseli only laughed and shook the raindrops out of her hair.

The little broken-down house was a fairly good shelter for them, but the little old man seemed very much frightened, so Urseli gave him some of her bread and cheese to eat. Although it was only old cheese and dry bread, he seemed to enjoy it, but, as he still seemed so unhappy, Urseli went over and put her arm round his shoulders, telling him to cheer up. Just as she spoke there was a really terrific flash of lightning, the thunder rolled and

roared at the very same moment, and Urseli fell to the ground and knew no more.

—4—

When she woke up she found that she was lying in an enormous bed between sheets of silk with blankets of velvet above them. The shine of gold all round was enough to dazzle her. A pretty young servant-girl stood by the bed and as soon as she saw that Urseli was awake she dropped her a little curtsey.

'You don't have to curtsey, dear!' Urseli said to the girl. 'There's some mistake! I'm only Foolish Urseli.'

The servant-girl only smiled. 'Would you like a bath?' she asked.

Urseli was not quite sure what to say. It was rather bewildering to find herself in such a grand place. However, she thought she had probably better do whatever the nice young servant-girl said, so she got up and, in the next room, was a lovely bath of gold full of scented water. Now the funny part was that the bath not only washed off the mud from the hollow that was still on Urseli's legs, but somehow it seemed to wash away all her foolishness too. She had always been a pretty girl and very good-natured, and now she was sensible as well.

The servant-girl brought her a beautiful dress, sat her down in front of a mirror, brushed and plaited Urseli's long fair hair, and she put gold shoes on her feet.

No sooner was Urseli ready and looking very pretty indeed, than a knock came on the door, and when it was opened there stood the handsomest young Prince you could possibly wish to see, and behind him were a lot of gaily dressed courtiers.

The Prince came forward and took Urseli's hand. Then he said solemnly to the courtiers:

'This is the girl who broke the spell and released me from a terrible enchantment.' Then he said to Urseli, 'I was the little ugly old man to whom you were kind, with whom you shared your bread and cheese and whom you comforted, and this palace is the little broken-down house in which we both tried to shelter from that thunderstorm.'

So now you know how Urseli became a Princess.

As for Katel and Gretel, they woke up as well but they just found themselves up by the summer dairy with the cows all round them piteously mooing to be milked, and the dairy in a terrible mess because the big cheeses hadn't been turned for such a long time and had got smelly.

But do you know? Those two girls really did clean the place up. They really did work for once in their lives. Though, in the end, they didn't marry Princes, they did marry two nice young farmers, and their sister, Princess Urseli, often had them to stay with her at the Palace.

The Sea Knight

Once upon a time, a fine ship was sailing on the seas that lap the cliffs and beaches that lie to the south of France. It was a beautiful day, the wind was fair, and round her the porpoises leapt and played, crossing her bows, crossing her stern, weaving in and out, while the sun sparkled on the water.

Now there was a rash young man among the crew, and what should he do but take out his cross-bow and, with an arrow, shoot at one of the porpoises. In a trice all the rest stopped their play and plunged to the bottom, while a long trail of blood from the wounded porpoise spread over the sea.

All at once the sky darkened, and, where all had been sunshine, now all was heavy cloud with a distant rumble of thunder, flashes of lightning, and a rising moan of wind. All that afternoon the storm grew stronger and stronger and they could see the waves breaking all round them. The moon rose and, at last, a fearful gust split the ship's main-sail.

Then the crew saw a very strange sight. In this time of waves and wind, in the very midst of the storm, a knight on horseback came riding up out of the sea. Then on he rode, towards the rolling ship and the terrified sailors.

'If you want to save your lives and to save the ship,' he cried against the howling of the wind, 'give me the man who wounded the porpoise!'

The captain and the crew wondered what they ought to do. Ought they to give up their shipmate to the demon horseman (for he seemed no less)? If they did not they might all perish in the storm.

Then it was that the young man himself—the one who had shot the arrow—gave them the answer, shouting from where he held to the rigging.

'I will go with you!' he cried out loudly to the horseman. 'I was a fool to shoot! I deserve to die!'

So saying, he leapt down on to the deck and from there on to the horse behind the rider, and, with that, the strange sea-knight galloped off, over the water, along the path of the moon, as though it had been a firm road.

On they went until they came to a high castle. The drawbridge was up, but the horseman didn't heed that but galloped over the water of the moat as easily as he had travelled over the sea.

Inside the castle yard the knight told the young sailor

to dismount and then he led him through the castle, through room after room. In the last one, on a magnificent bed, lay a young knight. He was very pale and blood still oozed out of a fresh wound with an arrow still stuck in it, an arrow that the sailor recognized. This was, he saw, the very arrow that he had aimed at what he had taken for one of the porpoises that was sporting round the ship.

'Pull out the arrow,' said the horseman in a stern voice. 'Then lay your guilty hand on the wound!'

The young sailor did as he was told, but his knees trembled and his hand shook as he tugged at his arrow. However, it was out at last, though a gush of blood followed it. Then he laid his hand on the wound and trembled again to see how the colour came back to the cheeks of the wounded knight who sighed at last and drew in a deep breath.

'He will live,' said the horseman who had risen out of the sea. Then with stern looks but without another word he led the sailor once more out of the castle.

Back to the horse they went, and when they had mounted once more, they galloped back over the sea down the path of the moon. At last when the dawn was beginning to break, in the grey light they began to see the ship. Her mainsail was down, still torn, but all the same she rode easily, for the crew had managed to re-rig her and the wind was now light, and the water calm.

The look-out man on deck gave a warning shout as, once more, he saw the magic horse galloping across the water. Quickly the crew tumbled up on deck and soon they were all giving thanks for the safe return of the young sailor who, with a mighty leap, sprang from the back of the horse on to the deck beside them. No sooner was the sailor safe than the strange knight and his horse sank beneath the waves.

From that time, till this very day, sailors believe that it is unlucky to hunt or to harm a porpoise.

Saturday, Sunday, Monday

In Italy there once lived a man and a woman who each had a son who was a hunchback. After a while the man's wife died and then the woman's husband.

Now the man often had to be away at work, sometimes for days at a time, and now that his wife was dead he didn't like leaving his poor little hunchback son all alone. So he thought that if he could only marry the widow, she would be able to look after both boys—his own son and hers—and the two poor, weak, sickly lads would be company for one another.

But all this didn't turn out as well as the man had hoped. He married the widow and she took good care of her own son—who besides being a hunchback, was a spiteful fellow. But when the man was out of the way, she behaved very badly to her poor little stepson, Thomaso, for she gave him very little to eat and made him do work which was far too hard for him.

One day in the autumn when Thomaso's father was away doing work in another village, the woman flew into a rage and fairly drove poor Thomaso out of the house.

What was the poor boy to do? He had a very sweet voice and sang beautifully, but that was all. He wasn't like other lads, strong and big, but hunchbacked and weak, so it wasn't going to be easy for him to earn his own living.

Walking was quite difficult for him and it began to get dark as he wandered away up into the mountains. Soon he was nearly crying. Presently, on the side of the mountain just in front of him, he saw a beautiful clump of sweet-chestnut trees. When he saw them he hoped that perhaps the chestnuts might be ripe by now, for he was very hungry.

Then he saw that there was a hut among the trees, and he began to feel afraid that someone might come out of it and drive him away. So he hid behind a rock and waited, hoping to find out if anyone was living in it. As he watched, the door opened and he saw a troop of tiny little men coming out of the hut. They took hands and began to dance, singing sweetly. Thomaso felt frightened at first until he noticed not only how nicely they were singing, but that every one of them was a hunchback—just like himself.

What tune they sang I don't know, but what I do know is that it was very pretty. It seemed, too, always to break off like a question that never got an answer; and when there was no answer, it began again. At last Thomaso was able to make out the words and, to his surprise, he found that there were only two of them, and the little men were singing the same ones over and over again:

'Sabbato
Domenica

Sabbato
Domenica'

which, you know, means:

'Saturday
Sunday

Saturday
Sunday'

Thomaso sat quite still and listened very carefully, and then, when he thought he had got the tune right, he chimed in quite loud and clearly in his sweet voice on just the right note.

'Lunédi,' he sang out, 'Lunédi'
(and that you know means 'Monday'.)

No sooner had he chimed in like this than the singing stopped and all the little men rushed to where he was hiding. Something strange seemed to have happened, for, as Thomaso looked about him, he saw that the little men looked much handsomer and when he stood up he found that his own hump had gone. No one had a hump any more and now, instead of being a weak, crippled boy,

Thomaso was tall and well grown. He felt light and happy, as he had never felt before. As for the little men, they were all round him, laughing and skipping about.

'Thank you, thank you, good people,' Thomaso cried out in delight.

'Not at all,' said the chief of the little men, taking off his small hat and bowing politely. 'It is WE who must thank YOU.'

'But I did nothing,' answered Thomaso. 'Tell me what I can do to show you how grateful I am.'

'You rewarded us before we could reward you,' said the little man.

'I don't understand,' answered Thomaso puzzled.

'You chimed in with your sweet voice, just on the right note, and went on with the melody, putting in just the right word. That is how you broke the spell that held us all.'

'Now that I'm strong and active, I could work for you,' said Thomaso who still felt he wanted to show how grateful he was in some way.

'Work at home if you like,' said the little man, shrugging his shoulders, 'but you won't need to.' Then with a sly look he gave Thomaso a little white stick. 'Go back and, if anyone tries to ill-treat you again, all you have to say is, AT HIM, GOOD STICK or AT HER, GOOD STICK, and you will soon see what it can do for you.'

The end of it was that Thomaso thanked them all again, took the stick and seeing that the moon now gave him light enough, went quickly back home, just as the little men had advised. This time he wasn't long on the way, for now he went jumping and running instead of only dragging himself along.

When he got to the house he managed to climb in without anyone hearing or seeing him.

Of course, next day, when the stepmother saw how he had changed, she wanted to know all about what had happened. Thomaso told her everything—except about the little stick.

'If you can do it, MY son can do it. He's got a far better voice than yours,' she said. 'Now tell us exactly the way you went and everything you did,' and with that she fetched in her own hunchback son so that he could listen too.

So Thomaso told his tale all over again, not leaving out anything—except about the stick. Then he said to his stepbrother:

'Be sure you listen very carefully to the tune, Brother. Everything seems to depend on coming in at exactly the right time and on exactly the right note.'

'I don't need singing lessons from you,' said the spiteful brother.

And that was all the thanks Thomaso got from either of them. However, he said nothing except that he wished his stepbrother good luck.

His stepmother was in a great hurry and she saw to it that her lad should set out early that very same evening.

He went in such good time that when he got to the grove of sweet-chestnut trees, it was still quite a long while before twilight. So of course he had to wait, for, as everybody knows, the Little People never come out in full daylight.

This lad, unlike Thomaso, was always one to grumble and find fault, so he soon got impatient. When at last the light began to fade, the troop of little men did come out of the hut just as before. Then they began to sing and dance. But, oh dear, this lad was in such a hurry that he hardly waited for them to sing their little tune over once, and never thought of giving himself time to learn it properly.

They were singing three words this time, instead of only two:

'Sabbato	Saturday
Domenica	Sunday
Lunédi	Monday.'

No sooner had they sung the last word than the impatient lad yelled out the word for Tuesday.

'MARTÉDI,' he shouted, 'Martédi,' quite out of time and tune.

When they heard this horrid screech, the little men all rushed angrily to where he was hiding.

'Horrible fellow! You can't sing! You shan't sing with us!' they all called. Then, as soon as they caught sight of him, they all picked up little sticks and began to pelt him with all their might. This wasn't at all what he had expected and, though the sticks were too small to hurt, he was so frightened that he made off home at once.

His mother was still out in the fields when she heard him coming and, with a big wooden rake still in her hand, she ran out to meet him.

'It was all a trap, Mother!' he shouted as soon as he was within earshot. 'Thomaso did it on purpose!' Then he told her the story, making out that the sticks had hurt him a great deal and that Thomaso had arranged it all. Hearing this she rushed off at once to find Thomaso, still with the rake in her hand.

'I'll teach you to treat your poor brother like that, you

evil creature,' she screamed. 'I'll break your neck for you,' and with that she went for poor Thomaso with the rake. But Thomaso was now as nimble as any other boy, so he easily dodged out of the way. Then, pulling out his little white stick he called out:

'AT HER, GOOD STICK!' At once the little stick leaped from his hand and began to beat the cruel woman. She was soon glad to beg for mercy and then Thomaso, who was always good-tempered, called back his little stick.

After that, neither she nor her spiteful son ever dared to behave badly to Thomaso again. He only did his fair share of the work about the place and got his fair share of food. As he worked among the vines or the olive trees he used often to sing to himself and what he sang was usually the tune he had learned from the Fairy Men. But, though he sometimes went up the mountain at twilight, to the sweet-chestnut grove and then sang the tune in his sweet voice, he never saw or heard them again.

The Tree with the Difficult Name

ONCE, LONG AGO, there came hard times in Africa and the animals had to wander about and look everywhere for food. At last, as they wandered, they came to a huge tree which was covered with delicious fruit. None of the animals knew the name of this huge tree. What they did know was that it is never safe to eat the fruit of a tree unless those who eat know its name.

However, they did find out something about this tree. It belonged to an old woman called Koko, and she lived quite a long way off. She of course was sure to know the tree's real name. Not just what sort of tree it was, but the name of that particular tree.

Well, they decided that the best thing to do would be for one of them to go to Koko and ask her. There was more fruit on a huge tree like that than one old woman could eat, so they thought that she would be sure to be willing to tell.

So the Hare was sent. It was a long way and he had to go down by the river. Sure enough, he found the old woman who was called Koko, and he said:

'Grandmother Koko! What is the name of your tree that stands in the bush? We animals are all dying of hunger but if only we knew the name we could eat the fruit and not starve.'

'Yes,' said Koko, 'I'll tell you the name of the tree and then you can ALL safely eat the fruit. All you'll have to do is just to stand underneath the tree and say—UWUNGELEMA.'

'U-WUNG-GELEMA!' repeated the Hare. 'What a difficult name! Thank you, Grandmother Koko. I won't forget it.'

As he went, on the way back, galloping very fast (you know how fast hares can run) he kept saying to himself U-WUNG-GELEMA, U-WUNG-GELEMA.' But after a while this hare tripped over a root, fell, and banged his head. When he got up he was quite dazed and the worst of it was that he couldn't remember the name.

'OOH . . . WU . . .' he said to himself, 'Yes! It was certainly something like that.'

When he got back to the village, all the animals said:

'Oh, little Mr. Hare, tell us the name of the tree!'

But all he could say was:

'*OO WU* . . . something like that!'

'Well,' they said, 'you're no good! We'd better send TWO messengers this time.' So they got the two big Elands to go.

The Elands went galloping down the path by the river and when they got to where she lived, Koko gave them the same answer. But to the Elands she gave one more bit of advice:

'When you're on your way back, O Elands, be sure not to look behind you!'

They thanked her for her help, but as they went, galloping very fast up the path again, the Elands heard a queer sort of noise in the bush, so that they felt as if something was after them, and one of them looked behind. So, the sad FACT was that when they got back to the village, they found they'd both forgotten the name of the tree.

'Well,' said the animals, 'now we've sent three messengers who all ran very fast! That doesn't seem to be much good! How would it be if somebody went by boat?'

So the Mongoose said he would try and, instead of going by the path, he took a canoe.

Koko gave him the same answer.

'U-WUNG-GELEMA!' said the Mongoose, carefully repeating the name after her. 'Thank you, Grandmother Koko!'

Then to the Mongoose she said one more thing:

'When you're on the way back in your canoe, don't eat or drink any of your provisions.'

But on the way back, the Mongoose had to paddle against the stream and at last he felt so faint and hungry that he ate a little bit of the food he'd brought with him. There! When he got to the village, he too had forgotten the name.

'We DESPISE you, Mr. Mongoose!' said the other animals. 'You're no good at all!'

'I shall go myself!' said the Lion. 'I'm the king!'

Well, Koko told the Lion the name and he repeated it over and over again all the way back, so as to be sure not to forget.

'UWUNGELEMA! UWUNGELEMA! UWUNGELEMA!' he kept on growling to himself, as he went along. Do you know what? He repeated it so often, that after a while, the word sounded to him like nonsense, and when he got back to the village, he was just as bad as the Hare.

All he could say was:

'It's something that begins with Ooooh . . . and goes on like Woo.'

Then a whole lot of animals tried. The big Buffalo went, stamping and blowing, and the little Gazelles went—very fast they went—but it was no use. At last ALL the animals had been, except the Tortoise.

'Let ME go!' said the Tortoise.

All the other animals looked at him. The Tortoise was the slowest of them all.

They shook their heads, but at last they said:

'You may as well try!' But they hadn't much hopes of such a slow, silly, little animal being any use.

So the Tortoise went and he went, on his little bent legs. Very slowly he went, but at last he got to where Koko lived.

'Grandmother Koko!' said he. 'Tell me how we may get the fruit. Tell me the name of the tree so that all we poor creatures may eat! ALL the other animals forgot what you said, so now we are all nearly starving.'

'Is that so!' said Koko. 'That is very sad! I expect they all went too fast! You must go back very slowly!'

'I ALWAYS go very slowly,' said Tortoise. 'I CAN'T go fast! That's the worst of it! I'm so afraid I shall forget what you tell me on the long, long way back!'

'I'll tell you what we'll do!' said Koko, nodding her head, 'I'll give you a little bell and as you go slowly along, the little bell will ring, and the sound of it will seem to you just like U-WUNG-GELEMA!' So then old Koko fastened a little bell to the Tortoise's shell.

Sure enough, as he went, very slowly along the path, the little bell rang all the time . . . U-WUNG-GELEMA . . . U-WUNG-GELEMA . . . U-WUNG-GELEMA . . . at least that's what it sounded like to the Tortoise. He began to feel very tired but, after a long time, he caught sight of the tree and saw that all the animals were still waiting under it.

The Tortoise was so tired that he could only just shout out, 'U-WUNG-GELEMA!'

But the others heard. Then they all shouted the word together and no sooner had they done that than all the lovely ripe fruit came pelting down!

Next morning, when they had all had a long sleep after their lovely feast, all the animals got up and then they all cried out:

'Mr. Tortoise shall be our Chief! He is the only animal who remembered the name of the tree!'

Why Rabbit Have Short Tail

ONCE, IN A LONG-BEFORE TIME before Queen Victoria come to reign over we, in dis country—dat's Jamaica—dere live ANANSI. Sometimes Anansi him spider and sometimes him man. One day Anansi him sittin' in him house and him rubbin' him stumick an smilin'.

Masser Rabbit him come along. Masser Rabbit him got lovely long tail in dem days and him got two lovely long ears, same as now.

Masser Rabbit say, 'How do?' to Anansi, and Anansi him say, 'How do?' to Masser Rabbit.

'Why you smilin' and rubbin' you stumick so pleased, Brudder Anansi?' ask Masser Rabbit.

'Cause me just eat such a nice fresh fish, Brudder Rabbit. Oh, dat fish taste so good.'

'You got liddle bit leff, Brudder Anansi? Let me taste?'

But Anansi, him is de sort of fellow NEVER give nothin' to no one. No, not even to him starvin' wife and family.

Anansi make out him so sorry, but him say him hasn't got even one fin, not even one bone, not even de fish tail leff, so him can't let Masser Rabbit taste how nice de fish was. Den him say: 'But tell you what, Brudder Rabbit. Wid the fine long tail you got, you catch fish yourself, easy.

If me show you how you can catch fish, you give me half what you catch?' Masser Rabbit him 'gree to dis. So Anansi tell him, all him got to do is dip him tail in Rum an' sit wid him tail in de sea an' den him pull out de fish, easy.

An' dat's just what Masser Rabbit do, an' de very first fish dat come 'long him a big one. Dat fish take juss one bite.

So dat's why Rabbit got short tail to dis day.

Bahmoo and the Frog

THERE WAS ONCE a tribe of river-Indians that had their home on one side of a certain big river that runs through forest and marsh in Guiana. At first nobody at all lived on the other bank of that river, but after what happened one day there were two tribes, one living on each side. Why are there two tribes? strangers would ask. Then, if it was evening and the right time for story-telling and if there was a story-teller about, and if the people who wanted to hear the story would promise to join in with the noises, this is the story that would be told. If someone is reading this story to you, you, who are listening now, must also promise to join in. The reason for this is, as the people of those two Indian tribes very well know, that one person can tell a story but one person can't possibly sound like a loud frog-chorus. Here then is the story.

Once upon a time just one tribe lived on one of the two banks of the wide river Essequibo. In the proper season of the year the young men used to go out to hunt for the large frogs that lived in hundreds in the marshes. This tribe was famous, not only for the huge size of their frogs and for the delicious way they cooked them over their camp fires, but also for the beauty of the girls of the tribe, so that suitors used often to come from far away in the hopes of getting one of these famous girls for a wife.

One of these suitors who came one year was a young man called Bahmoo and it wasn't long before he had his eye on one of the very prettiest of the girls.

Now this Bahmoo was a very good-looking young man so, on the very first evening, the pretty girl let him take her hand when they were dancing while she would not look at another young man who also wanted to court her. The fact that she seemed to like him made Bahmoo swell with pride, so much so that he determined, next day, when her brothers and cousins had offered to take him out frog-hunting, to show her, and his rival, and all the others, what a strong and clever fellow he was.

On the morning of the hunt all the young men who were going out painted patterns on their cheeks and dressed up by putting fresh toucan-feathers in their head-bands and each one took his weapon ready to go frog-hunting. But Bahmoo, though he put on his best feathers and head-band and though he painted some glorious patterns on his face and though he oiled himself all over till he shone, didn't seem to have any weapons.

'Take a club, O Bahmoo! If you haven't brought one you can borrow one,' the others said to him. 'See, this is a good one! Take this one. These frogs of ours really are big and if you want one for dinner you'll have to give it a hard blow.'

'Thank you very much,' says handsome Bahmoo in a proud voice. 'But I'll leave weapons to you! What I mean to do is to jump on to the first frog I see and then bend his head back and have him that way . . . I don't want to bother carrying a great heavy club through the marshes.'

'Just as you like, Bahmoo,' said the others and went on getting ready.

Now the Chief and ruler of all those hundreds and thousands of noisy frogs was not only bigger than all the rest but also he could understand every word that these river-Indians said. When he overheard Bahmoo doing all that boasting, doing it before the hunt had even started, the Chief Frog decided to teach him a lesson.

Did you notice that Bahmoo had said he would try his new way of frog-hunting with the very first frog he saw? Well, this was just what the Chief Frog had particularly noticed and he decided that he himself would be the first frog to be seen by Bahmoo. He came a little nearer to where the young men were standing talking and getting ready, and then he lay very quietly in a hollow of the marsh where Bahmoo was sure to see him, only a yard or two from the river. He lay there with his big frog eyes gazing up into the sky.

As soon as Bahmoo saw him, he began to creep stealthily towards him, thinking how lucky he was to have seen such a big frog so soon. Bahmoo wriggled along as quietly as he could on his stomach through the reeds and the squelching mud.

But though the enormous frog himself didn't stir, no sooner had Bahmoo begun to move than the frog-chorus began (this is where the audience always helps):

'*Boro ... ok! Boro ... ok! Bor ... oo!*' croaked the first frog. Then hundreds began:

'*Boro ... ok! Boro ... ok! Boro ... oo! ! !*' The noise was fearful—deafening. If you had heard it you might have thought it was hundreds of mad tractors all revving up and it seemed to come from all round Bahmoo. The other young men, who were used to the noise, were not, of course, in the least afraid of this hullabaloo. But Bahmoo couldn't help giving a start and letting out a little yelp: and also clapping his hands to his ears.

The young men in front of whom Bahmoo had just been boasting noticed this of course. They were all too polite to laugh out loud, but Bahmoo saw that they had noticed and wished he hadn't let them see that he'd had a fright. Though they were most polite, he felt quite sure that they were laughing inside. He knew too, that his new sweetheart was watching, so this made him determine all the more to do what he had boasted—he would catch and kill the first frog he saw, just with his bare hands.

So on he crept, and, in a moment, he had jumped at the Frog Chief, ready to catch hold of him and jerk his head back. But oh dear! This frog was so big and so slippery that, in a trice, it had slipped from under Bahmoo and soon it was the frog who was holding Bahmoo down with a pair of short front paws. Then, for one dreadful moment it seemed to Bahmoo that they were sailing through the air—then *splash!* They were in the river—the fast flowing river—with Bahmoo held tight to the frog's pale, slimy chest. The Frog Chief swam on and (just so as not quite to drown Bahmoo) he let him up for a gasp of air now and then, and every time Bahmoo came up he heard the ear-splitting noise of the frog-chorus (audience please join in):

'Boro . . . ok! Boro . . . ok! Bor . . . ooo!'

When they were out in the middle of the river and when the frog thought that it had ducked Bahmoo enough, it said to him in its croaking voice:

'Get on my back! Get on my b . . aa . . aa . . aak!' and with that it let go of him and Bahmoo felt himself being whirled away by the current and was glad enough to catch hold of the frog again and to climb on its back. When he was sitting there and had caught his breath, and got the hair out of his eyes, he heard the frog chorus (audience please!):

'Boro . . . ok! Boro . . . ok! Boro . . . ooo! ! !'

But he also heard another sound and, glancing back at the shore, he saw that the other frog-hunters were now shouting with laughter and indeed some of them seemed to be laughing so much that they were rolling on the ground.

Bahmoo was one of those people who hated to be laughed at, so now he began to struggle, wondering if he couldn't somehow get away from the frog.

'Twist his head off, Bahmoo!' the hunters shouted from the shore, laughing still more. But poor Bahmoo could not even get away because, as it swam with its strong hind legs, the Frog Chief was holding him by the ankles with its short front paws. Then, to make him still more ashamed, the that, in a trice, it had slipped from under Bahmoo and soon it was the frog who was holding Bahmoo down with a pair of short front paws. Then, for one dreadful moment it seemed to Bahmoo that they were sailing through the air—then *splash!* They were in the river—the fast flowing river—with Bahmoo held tight to the frog's pale, slimy chest. The Frog Chief swam on and (just so as not quite to drown Bahmoo) he let him up for a gasp of air now and then, and every time Bahmoo came up he heard the ear-splitting noise of the frog-chorus (audience please join in):

'Boro . . . ok! Boro . . . ok! Bor . . . ooo!'

When they were out in the middle of the river and when the frog thought that it had ducked Bahmoo enough, it said to him in its croaking voice:

'Get on my back! Get on my b . . aa . . aa . . aak!' and with that it let go of him and Bahmoo felt himself being whirled away by the current and was glad enough to catch hold of the frog again and to climb on its back. When he was sitting there and had caught his breath, and got the hair out of his eyes, he heard the frog chorus (audience please!):

'Boro . . . ok! Boro . . . ok! Boro . . . ooo! ! !'

But he also heard another sound and, glancing back at the shore, he saw that the other frog-hunters were now shouting with laughter and indeed some of them seemed to be laughing so much that they were rolling on the ground.

Bahmoo was one of those people who hated to be laughed at, so now he began to struggle, wondering if he couldn't somehow get away from the frog.

'Twist his head off, Bahmoo!' the hunters shouted from the shore, laughing still more. But poor Bahmoo could not even get away because, as it swam with its strong hind legs, the Frog Chief was holding him by the ankles with its short front paws. Then, to make him still more ashamed, the hiding in the river ready to make a fool of him again, for another he had had more than enough of being laughed at, and he was afraid that, when the girls saw him, they might be as bad as the young men and all start laughing as well.

So, all alone, Bahmoo wandered off down the river bank. He did not like it at all, in spite of there being so many fire-flies, for he could hear jaguars and leopards making noises that sounded much too much like laughing, and, far away, the miserable yells of a howler-monkey. Altogether Bahmoo felt very sad and lonely.

It was nearly dark, but at least there were the fire-flies; then the moon rose, and then, in the water, Bahmoo thought he saw a shadow. At first he was afraid that it might be the frog again, but instead of mocking croaks he heard a girl's voice softly saying his name:

'Bahmoo! Bahmoo!' called the shadow. 'Stretch out your hand! Quick! I'm being whirled past you!'

Then Bahmoo saw that the voice came from none other than the pretty girl with whom he had danced in the village. There she sat, half in and half out of the water, on a little raft, her long hair wet over her shoulders, and holding out her hand to take his.

Well, my chidren, the end of it was that Bahmoo caught hold of her hand and pulled her and her little raft ashore. She had brought some supper with her, well wrapped up, so that it had not got wet, and they sat down and ate it. Not long afterwards they were married. But though Bahmoo loved his wife very much, he could never agree to go back with her to her village, where they had laughed so much at him. No! the two of them stayed on the other side of the river.

So now you can understand why, to this day, there are two tribes—one on each side of the wide River Essequibo—and why one of these tribes hunts frogs, but the other does not.

Little Fish and Big Fish

In a river in Africa, not too far from here, and not too near, there lived many fish.

'If we can't think of something we shall all starve to death,' said an old experienced fish sadly. This he said because the river was so crowded.

All the river? No! Only one part.

When the old experienced fish had spoken, all the little fish who heard, all the fish who were so dreadfully crowded together, just in that one part of the river, all jumped up out of the water and then fell in again, *splash!*

By jumping and splashing like that they meant to say that they all thought that what the old experienced fish had just said was very sad and very true. Three more elders among the fish spoke:

'I wonder if Madam Eel has thought of something?' said the first.

'She's a clever one! She generally knows things,' said the second.

'Yes, eels hear more things than we do. They're just the right shape for getting into narrow cracks and listening to the news,' said a third.

Once more all the little fish jumped out of the water and fell back, *splash!* This time they meant that they thought somebody certainly ought to ask Madam Eel if she had perhaps thought of anything.

So the oldest fish, the experienced fish, called out:

'Madam Eel! We all hope that you will be so kind as to swim forward!'

The little fish, even though they were so dreadfully crowded together, just managed to make room for her. This was possible because eels are such a thin shape, just right for snaking their way through crowds. So when the Eel had wriggled forward to where the fish-elders were, she folded her fins ready for listening, for she could well see that the oldest fish meant to make a long speech. And so he did.

First, he paid her a great many compliments, for it is always best, if you want to get someone to do something, to begin with praise-talk. At last he came to the point: had Madam Eel noticed, he began, that down-stream, where the banks were high and close together—where the river was narrow and flowed in whirlpools—a monstrous fish had come to live? A frightful monster indeed, with huge eyes that shone in the dark, and sharp spines all along his back! Yes indeed! This monster of a fish had made his home in a dark hole under one of the rocks. And did Madam Eel know that any small fish, that was foolish enough to let the current take him too near, was instantly eaten by this shocking horror of a fish?

One such monster, the oldest fish went on, would have been bad enough, but, farther up-stream, lived an even more disgusting fish. This second up-stream giant of a fish had a double row of teeth and such enormous jaws that he could swallow things almost as big as himself. He was a truly dreadful beast who swam up and down day and night and never seemed to sleep at all. Any little fish that went near, however deep he swam under the water, was sure to be swallowed up. To add to the terror, whenever he swallowed an innocent little fish this dreadful creature always made a noise that sounded like '*Gouf!*'

'The consequence is, as you perhaps know, Madam Eel, that only a very short length of the river is now safe for us fish, and so we are getting more and more overcrowded.'

'Yes, and very short of food as well,' added a fish at the back.

'Have you thought about this dreadful state of things, dear Madam Eel?' asked the oldest fish.

'I have thought about nothing else for weeks,' answered the eel with a deep sigh.

'You are wise—you hear all the news—you are like a mother to us!' said another fish. 'Have you thought about what we had better do?'

'That is the chief thought in my mind,' said Madam Eel. 'I have thought of many plans! One is that we might leave this stream, cross over the marshes, and find another river. That might be all right if we were all eels, for *we* can wriggle about and travel quite well over any wet ground. But most of us are fish. So this plan won't do at all—except for me.'

The very idea of her going off like that was dreadful.

'For heaven's sake don't leave us, Madam Eel!' cried a mother fish. 'Remember that tomorrow a lot of new fish-eggs will hatch out!'

'How we are going to feed all these new baby fish, or even find swimming room for them, I can't imagine!' said another mother in a sad voice.

Then all the little fish jumped out of the water and fell back again, *splash!* By this they meant that they quite agreed with the two mother fish, and that, when all these extra eggs were hatched out, things would be even worse than they were now.

'Madam Eel, give us your true opinion! Do you consider that we are all going to die?' asked the old experienced fish. 'To die either by being eaten by one of the horrible monsters, by starving, or by suffocating because there won't be enough water for so many of us?'

'Well, I did think of one plan for avoiding it,' answered Madam Eel in a low voice. 'It will be dangerous for one of us, I'm afraid, and all of us will have to help a little.'

'We must try something!' said the oldest fish of all, 'so let us try Madam Eel's plan. Which fish will have the honour of volunteering to do the dangerous part? As you all know,' he went on, '*I* am too old!'

Not a fish said a word. But at last one at the back of the crowd spoke:

'Madam Eel hasn't explained what this dangerous part is. That is, no doubt, why no one has volunteered. Dear Madam Eel, you are like a mother to us! But don't you think that, as it's your idea, and as you can swim faster than any of us, you really ought to offer to do the dangerous part yourself?'

'If you will try, and if you are successful,' said the oldest fish of all quickly, 'you shall be our Chief from that time onward.'

At that all the little fish jumped out of the water and fell back again, *splash!* By this they meant that they thought that Madam Eel was exactly the right person to do the dangerous part and that she certainly ought to be their chief afterwards if she succeeded.

'But please explain your plan!' cried several middle-sized fish.

Madam Eel was silent. She was thinking. She was thinking that she herself could very easily escape by wriggling off to another river. On the other hand, it seemed to her sad that all the fish should be left to die. Also, she thought, she would very much like to be a Chief.

'Very well,' she agreed at last, 'but if I volunteer to do the dangerous part, you must all promise to do exactly as I say. I know how crowded you are, yet, when I give the signal, you must all press as close to the banks of the river as possible. Those who can, must even jump into the very shallow part among the reeds; those who cannot manage to do that must try their best to hide under stones. What I must be sure of is a wide passage of clear water in the middle of the river, perhaps for an hour or more.

Remember! The lives of all of us may depend on this!'

Then, without another word, Madam Eel began to swim through the crowd. Down stream she went towards the rocks, the whirlpools, the rapids and the down-stream monster.

'Oh, where are you going, Madam Eel?' all the older fish called out anxiously, as they began to swim along beside her, threading their way through the crowd as fast as they were able. 'You haven't even said what your plan is! You're surely not going to challenge that dreadful down-stream monster to a fight?'

'Oh, yes I am,' answered Madam Eel in a busy voice.

'Oh, do be careful!' called out all the fish-elders when they found that they couldn't keep up. 'Oh, what shall we do without you?'

Then all the little fish jumped out of the water and fell in again, *splash!* This time they jumped because, as she passed, they wanted to see the last of brave Madam Eel.

But as for her, with the water less crowded now, she went on swimming down-stream as fast as she could, without answering any of them.

Soon she had got quite clear of the crowd, to the dangerous part of the river, in sight of the brown rock under which was the cave of the horrible monster.

'Ohé!' she called out. 'Hey, you there! Ohé! Great Fish! Prince of this part of the water! Master-of-the-River-near-the-Rapids! Come out of your hole! I bring you a challenge to fight from the Emperor of the River!' She tried her best to make her voice sound as if she were telling the truth.

'A challenge to fight?' answered the great fish at last, poking his huge head out of the hole and rolling his great round eyes. 'What do you mean by that? Who are you anyhow? I've a great mind to eat you!' he went on, coming a little farther out of his hole.

'I don't advise you to try to eat me,' said Madam Eel, trying to sound very calm, but feeling rather nervous and keeping a careful eye on her enemy. 'If you try to eat me, you'll have to answer for it to the Emperor of the River who's much bigger and stronger than you!'

Would the big fish believe all these lies, she wondered? Anyhow she went on bravely:

'Do try to understand! I've been sent here by the Emperor of the River! His Imperial Highness would never forgive you if you tried to eat one of his messengers.'

'Never forgive me?' answered the great fish in a towering passion. 'How dare you talk like that? What do I care whether this fellow forgives me or not? As for his being the Emperor of the River, I never heard such nonsense! I'm just as much an Emperor as he is!'

'I wouldn't talk like that if I were you,' said Madam Eel, delighted to find that he believed her and that he was getting so angry. 'I don't know what the Emperor would say if he heard you!' She was pretending, of course, to be dreadfully shocked. 'He thinks that he is Lord of the Whole River, and just allows you to be master of this part and to call yourself a Prince——'

'Allows? Allows! That's too much!' bellowed the big fish, banging his tail on the water in a fury. 'Tell your ridiculous Emperor to mind his fins! I'm not going to be talked to like this! Tell him I'm going to swim up-stream and attack him!'

As the horrible great fish came further out of the hole, Madam Eel began to back away. She could see that he really was a monster; he had now raised the long row of spikes along his back, and the smaller row down his sides, so that he looked like a porcupine.

'My good fish,' said Madam Eel in a frightened-sounding voice, 'take care of yourself! If you try swimming up the river you'll meet my master in the middle, because, when I left him just now, the Emperor was getting ready to come down and teach you manners! He said if you didn't apologize, he'd kill you.'

'Swim off and tell your impudent master that I'm coming! I'm not going to be insulted! Tell him——'

But Madam Eel hadn't waited to hear any more. She was already off up the river, swimming like lightning, and giving the word to all the little fish to hide and to be sure to leave the way clear.

As soon as she saw the second great fish—the up-stream fish with the huge jaws and the double row of teeth, that lived at the bend of the river among the reeds—Madam Eel began to call out:

'Quick, quick my good fish! Oh, for goodness sake get ready! Your King and Master who lives farther down the steam, is very angry! He's on his way up to punish you.'

'King and Master! Punish! What's all this?' called out the great up-stream fish, swimming out from under the water weeds. Madam Eel could see that he was an immense creature, even bigger than the other, but she could see too, that he was cross already and quite ready to believe her.

'Who are you? And what are you talking about?' the big fish with the double teeth went on.

'I'm talking about the Great Fish that lives in his splendid palace by the rapids,' answered little Madam Eel. 'I've just seen him! He says he's the only Ruler here, and how dare you eat so many of his fish? He's in a furious temper. He'll be here in a moment, and he's sworn to kill you if you dare to resist.'

'Let him come!' bellowed the great-jawed monster. 'I'm not afraid of him or of anybody else! I shall eat what I please! I've a great mind to eat you—just to show your master what I think of him!'

'Oh, I wouldn't do that if I were you,' said Madam Eel. 'You'd far better just dive down to the bottom of the water and hide. You might manage to escape if you're careful. I shouldn't like to see you killed! Be quick and hide!'

'Hide? Me? Hide!' cried the furious monster, showing all his two rows of teeth. 'I'm bigger than he is!' He was so angry that he now leapt clean out of the water. 'I shall eat him! If anyone is going to hide it'll be him! You wait and see!'

But Madam Eel didn't wait. That fish hadn't finished shouting before she was off to make sure that all the little fish really had packed themselves along the sides and left a clear way up the middle of the river. It was all right! She

found that they were all hidden, and very much frightened as well.

Really it was no wonder that they were afraid, for by now the two enormous fish were swimming towards each other, swishing their huge tails and sending up great waves in the river. Their eyes glared like fire, their jaws were open. The second one was showing his enormous double row of teeth, while the sharp spines on the first one's back still stood up like giant hedgehog or porcupine spines, and all the while their strong fins and great tails beat the water.

What a battle it was! They hit and butted at each other, they banged at each other with their strong tails; they gave each other blows that made the little fish shudder. Soon

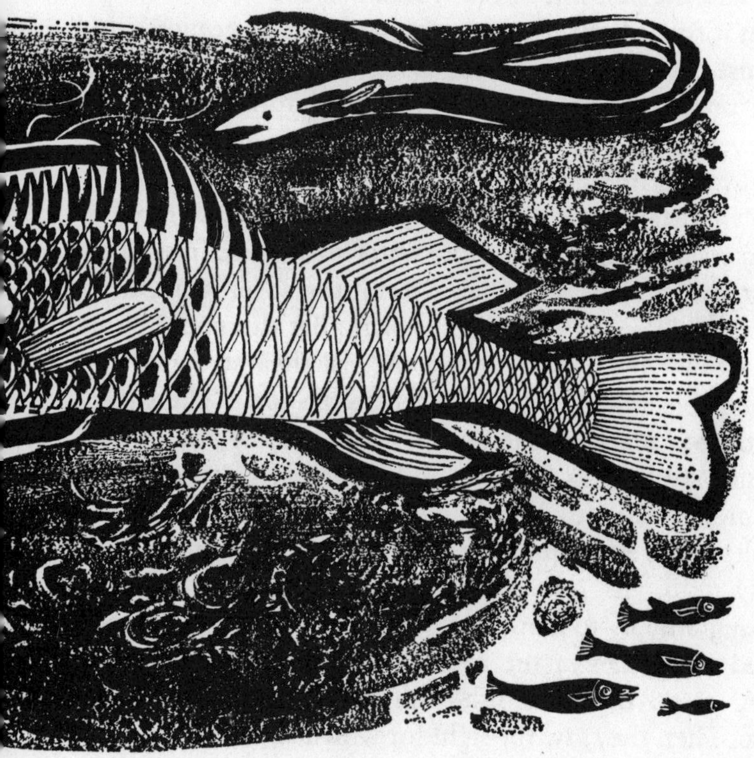

they were tearing at each other's scales and fins so much that, all round them, the water was stained with their blood.

First one monster and then the other seemed to be winning this furious battle. The up-stream fish with the double row of teeth was even bigger than the down-stream fish with the spines on his back, and had a bigger mouth. At last this up-stream fish opened his enormous jaws so wide that his mouth was like a cave. Just at that moment the first fish—the down-stream one who was covered with stiff spines—swam so furiously against his enemy that he couldn't stop himself and so he rammed his head right down the other monster's throat. It really seemed now that the huge up-stream fish had only to snap his great jaws and the first fish's head would be off.

But it turned out that this was just what he couldn't do, because the long row of stiff spines down the other fish's neck prevented him from closing his mouth. So the two fish were locked together! Madam Eel and the little fish, who were watching in terror from the shallows, saw how each monster tried in vain to get away and how each of them tried to jump out of the water so as to be free. They struggled and beat with their tails till the water foamed. So fiercely did they fight that it was plain that this couldn't go on and that neither could win. At last their struggles got quite feeble and then they floated to the top of the water. In another moment the current was carrying the two of them away, rolling them about like helpless bits of wood, for, in their fury, each had killed the other!

When they were quite sure that both their enemies were really dead, the little fish, who were still very nervous, began gradually to come out of hiding, and, as the current rolled the bodies of the two big fish farther and farther down river, the little fish—still frightened—swam after them. Then they saw the sight for which they had hoped—

the two horrible creatures were being washed away. Down over the rapids they went and into the whirlpool, never to be seen again.

After they had seen this excellent sight, all the little fish turned round to greet Madam Eel and, in order to show their joy, to thank her and to tell her that now she was their chief, they all jumped out of the water together and fell back again, *splash!*

So now you know how it was that in that river the eels became Chief of all the Fish.

3

The Story of Prince Ahmed

—1—

THERE WAS ONCE a Prince who lived in Morocco, who was the handsomest young man you could ever hope to see.

Even as a young boy this Ahmed had been so beautiful that his father thought to himself that, when he grew up, Love would be a great danger to his son. Thinking about this, his father fancied that, when he was grown, Ahmed would very likely refuse to marry the Princess that the King his father would choose for him. But, suppose, thought the King, that Ahmed had never seen any other woman, then he would probably be obedient, and would marry the one that had been chosen for him.

So this is what the father did. He called for a wise man, the wisest old man in all Morocco, and he told him that he was to teach his son and look after him, but that he must promise to allow himself to be shut away with his pupil.

Then, for the two of them, the King built a splendid palace. It was large and surrounded by beautiful gardens full of shady trees, and lawns, and bubbling streams, but Ahmed and the old sage were never allowed outside the garden walls. Pupil and teacher were waited on by black slaves, and no woman was ever allowed to come in.

From his wise old tutor Prince Ahmed learned many things; to read and to write, to understand algebra, how the stars wheel about the night-sky, and many other things such as any child might learn, but also something much stranger. His old tutor taught Ahmed the language of the birds, so that, when he heard their songs, he could understand everything that they said and could speak to them in their own language.

It was a strange life for a boy, for the only human people Ahmed had ever seen were his old tutor with his long white beard and the black slave-men who waited on them.

One spring, when the roses bloomed in the palace garden, and when, in the evening, many nightingales sang in the trees, and when Prince Ahmed was leaning over the balustrade of the terrace in front of the palace, a Dove came and perched in a pomegranate tree that grew down below. The Dove began to coo and the Prince listened.

'Love!' cooed the Dove. 'Love! Truly it is the torment of one, but the joy of two.'

'I know nothing about Love,' said the Prince with a sigh.

'You know nothing about Love? How sad!' answered the Dove in her soft voice. 'For you are young, and now it is the spring-time of the year. Sad! Sad!'

'Are women beautiful? I have never seen a woman.'

'Woman are beautiful just as you are beautiful. But they are different. I know where the most beautiful of all women is to be found. She is young with soft black eyes, her hair is long and her step is as light as that of a gazelle.'

'But if you know, O Dove, tell me where this lovely creature is to be found!'

'She lives far away in a palace that stands in a delightful garden, by the banks of a stream that murmurs through green lawns. But the walls of this palace are as high as those that are round your own palace. So you could not enter, my Prince! Only the winged birds can enter.'

'And you can go back and forth, sweet Dove?'

'Yes,' said the bird and began preening her feathers.

'O pretty Dove,' said the Prince at last, 'fly to this beautiful maiden, and tell her that in this palace also there lives a prisoner. Tell her how I have lived. Tell her that I have never had a companion and that my heart longs for her.'

The Dove watched Ahmed and saw that he was in earnest. She put her pretty head on one side to consider.

Ahmed wondered if she meant that she did not intend to help him.

'But how shall I tell her of your heart's longings?' said the Dove and then Ahmed remembered that, since the Dove could not speak the language of mortals or the maiden understand the language of birds, he must write. This he did, on a tiny strip of parchment, and the Dove showed him how to tie the scrap under her wing.

One day passed, two days and then three days passed, and every evening, at the time when he had first spoken with the Dove, Ahmed would go out on to the terrace, and he would lean his elbows on the balustrade whose stones were still warm from the sun. Then he would sigh, listen to the nightingales, and wonder if he would ever see the Dove again. But the pomegranate tree remained empty, though elsewhere in the garden everything was the same and the fireflies flitted and the roses bloomed.

At last, on the fourth evening there was the Dove again, but it seemed to Ahmed that her feathers were ruffled and that her eyes were no longer so bright. She did not perch on the tree this time but flew down close to him and rested on the balustrade. Ahmed put down his hand gently, and, under one wing, he found a little scented roll of parchment. He took it out, but before he opened it he said:

'Poor Dove! What ails you?'

'The flight was long! I am almost dead of thirst,' answered the bird and hung her head.

The Prince at once clapped his hands. One of the black slaves came and he told the man to bring water, but before he could get back the Dove had flown away and, though that night he heard her soft voice in the garden, Ahmed never saw or spoke with her again.

When he saw that she had gone, the Prince looked at the little parchment that she had brought and perceived that it was scented with attar of roses and dusted with gold and that on one side was a picture and on the other side a message written in a beautiful Arab script:

'Oh Prince!' it said. 'Because of the Dove I know your tale. But Fate is against us, for surely we can never meet. A troop of suitors has come, called here by my father the King; soon a splendid great tournament will be held to decide who is to be my husband!'

On the other side of the parchment was an exquisite miniature, the portrait of a beautiful young Princess; she had eyebrows like moths' wings, teeth like pearls, lips like pomegranate seeds and her thoughtful eyes were large.

Now in all his life Ahmed had never seen a beautiful maiden, still less one as beautiful as the Princess in the picture.

'The Dove spoke truly,' thought he. 'For now that its arrow has entered my heart I can feel that Love is indeed the torment of one.' Then putting his hand on his sword he added, 'Now I must find out if it is also true that it can be the joy of two.'

—2—

So that was how it came about that young Prince Ahmed determined to get away from the palace. He lost no time, but that very night, when the old sage was safely asleep, he managed to escape from the slaves who guarded him and to climb over the high wall.

Now the Dove had told Ahmed that the garden of the Princess was far away in Spain and that she was the daughter of a Moorish king who had his palace in Toledo. So Ahmed made his way to the coast and there he was lucky enough to find a ship which soon landed him on the shore of Spain. Here again he was lucky, for, almost at once, he managed to find a merchant who was just then ready to set out across the mountains with a string of mules with merchandise for Toledo. Many merchants indeed were going that way because of the great tournament. They hoped not only to see it, but to sell their silks, rose-water, spices, sweet-smelling gums, coffee and scented leather.

As soon as they got in sight of the high hill on which Toledo stands, Prince Ahmed saw that tents had sprung up all round the city walls and that great crowds of splendid warriors were all going that way. The merchant's string of mules often had to leave the road because the bodyguard of some important knight came clearing a path for him:

'Make way! Make way!' they cried. 'Room for our noble Master!'

Now as you know, Ahmed had never been outside the palace and its gardens. True, he had been taught to ride, to draw the long-bow and how to use lance, buckler and sword. But, as you also know, he had escaped. He had escaped over a high wall in the middle of the night, and now he had neither horse, armour nor weapons, and little money to buy even food. So what was he to do? With bare, empty hands how could he join in the tournament or tilt against the other suitors?

Poor Ahmed, as he sat that evening, leaning against the high walls of the city of Toledo, and as the night began to fall, he thought how powerless he was and how he had mismanaged everything and he wept.

Presently, he saw, in a tree above him, a white Owl.

'Who-o are you-uu-u?' cried the Owl, as owls often do.

'I am Prince Ahmed,' answered the Prince.

The Owl had, naturally, not really expected to get an answer to his question and was very much surprised to find a young man who could speak his language, so he flew down nearer, floating on his broad noiseless wings, and he stared at Ahmed with his great round yellow eyes.

'Why are you so sad?' asked the Owl.

Then Ahmed told him the whole story, just as you've heard it here, how he had run away from the palace in which his father kept him with his old tutor, all because the

Dove had brought him news about a lovely Princess, and how now, although he had managed to get to Toledo, it had been only to find his journey would probably be quite useless.

'I have neither horse nor spear, sword nor armour, O Owl!' ended he.

Then the Owl spoke again:

'In among the steep rocks around Toledo, in the face of a high cliff, there is a secret cave, a cave which is known only

to us owls. The entrance is hard to find and is narrow and dark, but inside there hangs the lamp which burns everlasting oil. I advise you to go to this cave.'

'What shall I find there?' asked Ahmed.

'You will see what you will see!' answered the bird.

Beg as he would, the Owl would tell the Prince no more. Though the Owl could not only fly but could see very well, it was now too dark for Ahmed to walk among such crags. But when the first cold light of dawn began to make things visible, the Owl, silently floating along in front, led him up a winding path and to the hidden mouth of a cave. There with a last, loud, '*Too Whit! TOO WHOO!*' the bird left him.

Inside the rock it was very dark, but Ahmed felt his way along a twisting passage. Sure enough, when he turned a sharp corner, the passage opened out into a cave and there hung the lamp, as the Owl had said. On an iron table lay a complete suit of armour, leaning against it was a lance and a sword, and, strangest of all, beside it stood a beautiful Arabian horse which stood perfectly still as though it were made of stone. Ahmed looked at the armour and saw that it was as bright as if a knight's squire and pages had newly scoured it. He saw that the lance was keen, the sword sharp, and that the helmet was set with precious stones. But far the most wonderful thing was the horse, for it was not stone, but flesh and blood and had a coat that shone like satin. As soon as Ahmed laid a hand on its neck, the horse began to breathe, then it pawed the ground, and at last it rolled an eye at Ahmed and gave a neigh so loud that it seemed to shake the walls of the cave.

—3—

Thus it was that, that very day, as soon as the sun was up, Prince Ahmed was able to go to the tournament riding on a splendid Arab horse and wearing armour finer than that of any other suitor.

But though Ahmed looked so splendid, the other Princes drew away from him. They whispered together saying that he was a stranger, that the Moorish King had not invited him and that even if he really did come from Morocco as he said, he had no right to fight and tilt for the hand of the lovely Princess.

One huge black-bearded Moorish knight wasn't content with drawing away and whispering. He rode up to Ahmed and mocked him; he told him loudly that he was only a baby, not fit even to tilt and far less fight, with real men. Ahmed said nothing, but he noticed that, at the sound of these words, his horse cocked his ears, trembled and snorted.

Ahmed indeed hardly heard these insulting words for he had just caught sight of the lovely Princess of the picture who was now sitting with her ladies ready to watch the tilting. Then, in a moment, the trumpets blew for the tournament to begin and Prince Ahmed found that chance had decided that he and Black-Beard who had mocked him were to be the first to ride and tilt against each other. So the two knights saluted each other, trotted their horses to their stations, put their lances in rest and then galloped full tilt against each other.

At the first touch of the magic lance from the cave, the huge black-bearded knight was knocked clean out of his saddle and on to the ground.

The Prince would, according to the rules, have pulled up his horse to let Black-Beard get to his feet. But, to his dismay, he found that his horse had no idea of letting him do that. Quite the contrary! Jumping lightly over the man who lay there helpless in his heavy armour, the horse charged into the closest part of the waiting crowd of suitors. Ahmed, who still had his lance in rest, could do nothing but hold on to it, and it overthrew everyone it touched. The horse was not content with one charge, but the young Prince was carried pell-mell across and across the field, strewing it with wounded suitors and their followers, so that soon there were riderless horses everywhere.

'Stop, stop!' Ahmed cried to the wilful horse, for this was

not proper conduct at a tournament and he feared that this was not at all the way to win a lady's love. He could see indeed that his lady's father, the King, was growing very angry.

'Seize the unknown knight!' cried the King.

So his mounted guards all drew their scimitars and rode against Ahmed, but this was no use either. They were each sure to be thrown from their horse as fast as they came up to him.

When the King saw what was happening to his guards he became more furious still. He had not meant to join in the tournament, but this was serious, so he quickly threw off his royal robes, took his splendid buckler and lance, mounted his royal charger and himself rode against Ahmed.

The Prince was now more worried than ever. He did not at all want to topple over this angry King, for he was hoping to marry his daughter and would need his consent. But it was no use. The magic horse was impossible to control. With its ears laid back and mane streaming, it galloped off to get a good run, then it turned and charged back and, in a moment, the King himself, crown and all, was rolling in the dust and his riderless horse was trotting quietly away.

Now you must know that this tournament had begun in the cool of the morning, but now it was near noon. Just as the sun was going to rise to its highest point in the sky, the Arab horse began to behave as if it was falling into the grip of some strange power. Now, instead of charging about, the horse, still giving Ahmed no chance to dismount, nimbly leapt the barrier that had been put round the tournament-ground. Then it galloped down the steep main street of Toledo and plunged into the broad river Tagus that runs at the foot of the hill. Swimming strongly, in spite of its rider in the heavy armour, the horse reached the other side where it galloped on, up the winding path and carried Prince Ahmed back into the cavern. At last another change came over it, and it seemed to be a statue once more, cold, quiet and utterly still.

Ahmed dismounted, but what was he to do now? Quite unwillingly he had wrecked the tournament, he had nearly killed the King, and had seen no more of the lovely Princess than a few glimpses as the wild horse galloped.

But she had seen him, and the arrow of Love had wounded her just as it had wounded Ahmed. But what was she to do?

What she did was this. Next day she pretended to be ill. This was to gain time, for she was now more than ever unwilling to marry any of the other suitors. Her pretence was believed and soon she was surrounded, no longer by suitors, but by doctors and physicians—tall, grave men, with huge turbans and long beards, who brought her broths and herbs and magic charms and tried, of course quite without success, to cure her. A word or two from Prince Ahmed would have made her better, no doubt, but he was hiding in the cavern, hiding from the King's guards who, if they had found him, would probably have cut him down on the spot.

On the third night, when he had crept out after dark to try to find some food, the white Owl found him, and told him the news of the Princess's pretended illness.

'What am I to do, O Owl?' asked Ahmed when he had told the bird what had happened.

'Pretend to be a doctor, O Prince! Go disguised!' said the Owl. Then the bird went on to tell him how he could manage best.

Ahmed decided to follow the Owl's advice and back he went into the cavern. Once more when morning came, he put his hand on the horse's neck, once more the horse came to life, though for all these days it had seemed like a horse of stone. This time Ahmed left the cavern as the sun rose, with only the horse, which he led. He took no armour, sword, nor lance with him.

Riding down the path and then leaving the horse tethered by some trees near the broad river Tagus, the Prince, who had disguised himself so that he looked both old and wise, went on foot to the palace. There he told the attendants that he was a famous doctor and that he, and he alone, could cure the sick Princess. They believed him and led him in. There she lay, white, still and silent. But sure enough, at a word from the new doctor she sighed, she sat up, she shook back her long scented hair and fixed her splendid black eyes upon him. But Ahmed signed to her to be careful, and, pretending that it was a charm, he slipped a message into her hand.

That night he and the magic horse were waiting for her outside the palace. The Princess stole softly out to them, and, in a moment, Ahmed had stooped and lifted her safely to his saddle-bow. Swift as an arrow the magic horse was off, swiftly it carried the lovers back to the palace in Morocco where Prince Ahmed had lived so long with only his old tutor and the black slaves.

And there it was that he and his Princess found that the Dove had spoken true and that, though Love is the torment of one, it is the joy of two.

As for Ahmed's father, he learned another truth, which is that neither Love nor magic horses have any respect for fathers. But Ahmed's bride was so lovely and she spoke so sweetly that he soon forgave both her and Ahmed. As for the horse, it became a horse of stone, and though Ahmed would often put his hand on its neck and though, after a while, the Princess would put their baby son to sit on its back, stone it remained.

LOVE LIKE HELL

HENRY NORMAL

INN

INTRODUCTION

This is the third edition of 'Love Like Hell' and probably the last.

Extra to the changes in the second edition there are now a further 7 poems. THE POEM I HOPE I SHALL NEVER WRITE CALLED ENGLAND and THE ACCIDENTAL DEATH OF A CAT, first appeared in a limited print run booklet entitled 'Do you believe in carpetworld?'. The other additions: THERES ALWAYS ROOM IN SPOON, THE FIRST FRACTURE OF INNOCENCE IS THE HATCHING OF ALL REGRET, PRAGMATIC ROMANTICISM and St VALENTINE'S RESTS NOT ON THE CALENDER BUT IN THE HEART are all new poems. As you can see my titles have improved if nothing else.

It's perhaps worth restating here the final words to the back cover of the first edition -

> 'Don't be put off by the title,
> LOVE LIKE HELL is not a melancholy observation
> but an appeal to passion'.

Dedicated to my three sisters, Linda, Valerie and Angela

ALL POEMS by HENRY NORMAL
Flat 15, Marella Ct., 62 Delaunays Rd.,
Crumpsall, Manchester, M8 6RF.
Tel: 061 795 8684

a twist in the tale

COVER by PETE RAMSKILL

FIRST EDITION PUBLISHED (1988)
SECOND EDITION PUBLISHED (FEBRUARY 1990)
THIRD EDITION PUBLISHED (JULY 1990)

by A TWIST IN THE TALE PUBLISHING,

LIST OF POEMS

LOVE LIKE HELL

LOVE LIKE HELL

I have this theory that when you die your whole life is re-run like a sensorama video and you have to sit through it all again, every second, unedited, in a room with every friend and every relative that's been in the least bit involved. Now depending on what sort of life you've led this could be Heaven or it could be Hell. Think about it, everyone's going to see those private moments, those very private moments: farting in the bath; wiping bogies down the side of the armchair; every second of indulgent masturbation.

All the pathetic lies you told exposed for all to see; all the naff chat-up lines you used when you were a teenager, and still used later; all the places you had sex when you still lived at home. The things you did to get by; the way you justified it all to yourself and every really dumb-arsed no-balls shit-for-brains mistake you ever made you'll have to watch yourself make again.

But then

maybe

there'll be those moments of rare beauty; the moments of tenderness; the times you cried because you messed up; the things you meant to say; the questions in the mirror; the promises you made when you first held your own child; the nights you comforted another's despair; the time your lover's face glowed like beauty on fire; the times you said "I love you" and believed your love would outlive the universe. The time you first held in your stomach thinking no-one would notice, and the regret in your eyes when you feared you were getting old. When you couldn't sleep one night and lay awake sweating and praying you didn't die before doing something, something, just something.

It's only a theory, and in my more optimistic moods I like to think that maybe there'll be a pause and a rewind for the good moments, and a fast forward for the rest.

FIG. 1 AND FIG.2 DISCUSS THE VALUE OF COLD SEX

Diagrams don't have headaches
never have a lousy day
are never self-conscious and
are always in perfect shape
diagrams don't mind sex cold
their sole purpose is to breed
closeness and affection
they don't really need
diagrams are never hurt
and
diagrams never bleed

ANIMATE PASSION

Romance pales in the predictable

Now is
always the time for something irrational

THE HOUSE IS NOT THE SAME SINCE YOU LEFT

The house is not the same since you left
the cooker is angry – it blames me
The TV tries desperately to stay busy
but occasionally I catch it staring out of the window
The washing up's feeling sorry for itself again
it just sits there saying "What's the point, what's the point?"
The curtains count the days
Nothing in the house will talk to me
I think your armchair's dead
The kettle tried to comfort me at first
but you know what it's attention span's like
I've not told the plants yet
they still think you're on holiday
The bathroom misses you
I hardly see it these days
It still can't believe you didn't take it with you
The bedroom won't even look at me
since you left it keeps it's eyes closed
all it wants to do is sleep, remembering better times
trying to lose itself in dreams
it seems like it's taken the easy way out
but at night I hear the pillows
weeping into the sheets.

PUPPY LOVE – A DOG'S LIFE?

Whatever happened to little Julie Bowers? She was classy.
I'd never seen anyone so clean, she must have washed every day. Proper leather school satchel with the straps and buckles and everything, just like in the Bunty comics. Not that I read Bunty comics, sometimes I cut out the outfits on the back cover.
Luckily around this time I discovered masturbation, so I no longer had to hang from playground equipment to achieve that pleasant tingling sensation in my groin.
But Julie Bowers was above all that, she was classy.
She was the kind of girl who would never fool around behind the library curtains. I was just a scruffy kid with snotty sleeves and hand-me-downs from an older sister, our love could never be. She lived in the posh part of the council estate where the houses had hedges too thick to dive through. She was unattainable, a Goddess.
She had the complete set of felt-tip colours, the full range with the light and dark brown. To her jigsaws were fun. She entered all the Blue Peter competitions and she could read Look And Learn without faking it.
She was classy alright, something of a playground intellectual and I respected her mind, though in my weaker moments I just wanted her to snog me to a state of total exhaustion. That seductive overbite, the cute turned-up nose, her neat ponytail, pleated skirt and those knee length white socks, she knew how to drive a boy wild.
Yes she was classy, mind you round our way any girl who ate with her mouth closed was considered classy.
What could I do? I tried to drown my sorrows in Taunton's cider but developed chronic flatulence instead. Were these really to be the happiest days of my life?

ONLY CHRISTMAS AND BIRTHDAYS BRING DEATH THIS CLOSE

Overnight
you have grown old
and though spite is no spur to succeed
in the absence of caress it can suffice

Only yesterday with hair dye and vitamins
you boasted you had cheated time
but now
it is the last dance of the party and
the prospect of a taxi home alone
rises like a flush within your cheeks

Years you wasted slip through the
doorway giggling together adolescent
Clear skin and eyes so bright
and always with partners that look such fools, but young
It is not them you hate but their youth
There is no individuality in this attraction merely the
aesthetics of innocence

and you, clinging to that one chance
force yourself into the night air before
the indignity of being the last to leave

I have seen you in the morning
lost in some mundane task
unaware of my presence
There is a subtlety of emotion that wisps around your eyes
You hesitate behind each door
    What worries you most is the loss of appetite
Where once you were so sure,
    diplomatic farewells have beaten back your pride
Where once you were curious,
    the nakedness of longing has sought to scar your faith
breathe still
breathe still
no whim of nature will chill your soul tonight

there are traditions that carry the truth of seasons
there are books that will outlast technology
we are old friends you and I
rest your fears against these words
it'll be alright
it will be alright.

LET'S PRETEND

Let's pretend we're both drunk and you're not married
and I'm not courting that girl in the kitchen and nobody
can see us and we don't know what we're doing and you put
your hand down my trousers whilst I lick your nipples and
if anyone comes in and finds us we were only pretending.

And because it's dark we can pretend to fumble about and
grope at each others crotch and buttocks and you can drape
your knickers over my head whilst I bend you over the chair
and if people should say anything we can pretend it was only
innocent party games and when we sink to the ash stained
carpet exhausted and unkempt we can pretend it was great and
even that we share something special and then you can go back
to your husband and I to my girlfriend and pretend.

LOVE TURNED GREEN

She inflicted her love like a wound
and only with her hand laid on the wound
and only when it wept did she have faith in her love
it was a love that cowered in doorways
a love that talked in accusations
where the words "I love you" became a threat
and where love hung like terror over every chance remark.

THIS LAND OF EQUAL OPPORTUNITY

A patch of dirt on his mother's skirt he clings on to save his life
A passenger in her frustration dragged past the age of five
Not for him the fairy land
He's taught right and wrong by the back of the hand
His life is planned inbred at birth
The urban waste of a council estate his first taste of Mother Earth
Told to sit as soon as he could crawl
The fiction in the picture books don't fit his life at all
And his mind begins to wonder what lies behind the high school wall
His mother can't wait to placate him
She lays more sugar on his dummy
"Work harder" says his father, "you too could soon earn money."
If it wasn't so sad it might just be funny
He sees his parents lie and cheat
Then discovers the other face they displace on the street
He's being taught the basic language of corruption and deceit
Used as a hostage in their petty rows
Abuse of a child is not reviled in the marriage vows
So thrown against the fridge in silence he looks
At violence and pain unknown in his kiddies story books
Now they've traded the dummy for the TV
The teacher asks him what he wants to be
He never mentions a job on the factory floor
But then neither did his father some thirty years before
With dreams scraped from the TV screen
And a start in life best forgot
In this land of equal opportunity
What chance has he really got?

THERE'S ALWAYS ROOM IN THE HEARSE ON THE WAY BACK

Joseph plays the percentages.
He can be eyeing up four women in different parts of
the same room.
He takes his data day diary literally.
A wall chart of his sperm level would read like a cardiac arrest.
To him Love is a dog with six legs.
Relationships, just things that crash in the night.
Loyalty, a free fall from infatuation to indifference.
From the erotic to the erratic.

There is a need to prove that he can still compete.

To Joseph
Nature gives no time to niceties.
Forever, comes with in-built obsolescence.
There always appears a point in coupling when he feels like
he's stuck next to someone on a long coach journey having ran
out of conversation.

In despair, it is of course the things we don't say that shout
the loudest.
Joseph mutilates his every hour.
I don't believe he chooses to be ugly
it is merely an ailment
a sickness of the spirit.

Joseph's crime is that of cowardice.
He has spent his whole life running with the eye of the storm
and destiny seems such a big word for such a small return.

Cranking up suspense in adolescence
  the pivot and swerve
  the running of the escalator
  carnal desire his internationalle
Joseph shys away from the need of a meaning

For the ultimate taboo is to be lonely.
  even for a second
  and so to fail
  to be an object of pity
  to be a loser
and cliches become cliches for a reason
no-one, but no-one, loves a loser.

It is to strands of this
he ties his final submission.
  Hoping as mortality yawns.
  Hoping as the sediment thaws.
  Hoping as the essence pulls immediate to his breath
that his lies
are lies
after all.

LOVE BY LIST

You're new to my list of acquaintances
let us list the things we have in common
I like your lists – here are a list of good points I've spotted
here is a list of things for us to say, and a list of other lists that
will come in handy.

I love you, see under list no.14
for response.
You are not responding correctly
have you read your lists? Here is a
list of things you are doing wrong.
Here is another list, you will see some
items have been duplicated.

I'm afraid I've lost the list with
your good points, but it's OK
I'm too busy keeping all these
lists together.

I'm going to have to
take you off my list of active
relationships, still don't worry
I have a list for you
we can put you here under failures.

THE TROUBLE WITH THERESA

Theresa wants desperately to be loved
She flings her arms around the world
as if to say "I love you, why won't you love me?"
Theresa tries too hard to be accepted
Within minutes of meeting her
she'll have told you her entire life story
she'll have squeezed your arm
she'll have bought you a drink.
Theresa sees all her own faults but no-one else's
she needs constant reassurance
she finds relationships never last but
she's never the one to break up; no matter what
she clings on and clings on tight,
as if to say "I love you, why won't you love me?"
The trouble with Theresa is she desperately wants to be loved
that's the trouble with Theresa
that's the trouble.

NEED

If need was currency
who could buy you from me?

THE POEM I HOPE I SHALL NEVER WRITE CALLED ENGLAND

The poem I hope I shall never write called England has 60
million pairs of sensible shoes, written in co-ordinated
pastels, it smiles a Dale Carnegie smile between the lines of
500 miles of dark blue pinstripes.

With a meal ticket for the gravy train you pay 6 Hail Mary's
and say you are just trying to get through, but is it ever
enough just to get through?

Dehumanised by the doberman mentality, behind the turrets of
the neighbourhood watch, I see the dust on the lustre of the
Emerald Isle and small swastikas on the latest liberty prints.
To the court of St James - never mind the product feel the
lifestyle. The writing on the wall bids you welcome to Hotel
Earth where as precious as poetry you hold up your life to the
light and find it ornate like a hollow case or a pale thin
complexion, until shards of conscience kick sand in your suntan
lotion and you suffer with all the political depth of a
designer sweatshirt. It's the gospel according to St Michael
carrier bags. I breath in - Whig history and the uncivil list,
Cathedral cities wringing their hands, invisible earnings and
the bank of opinion tells me throw another miner on the
barbecue.

Meanwhile ......
Meanwhile ...... back at reality ......
Meanwhile ...... back at reality ...... the divisions blister

I see old men asking for ten pence outside multi-million pound shopping centres, cardboard box bedouins bowing to the power of the rota blades, bamboo Babel and the American wet dream. Diluting to taste, Gazza attempts the futility of the Sun crossword, I drank the world T shirt, unzips a grin, draws a Hitler moustache on a Harrier jump jet, Benny Hill burgers for breakfast, going down for the third time, sucking plankton, I breath in - Bingo culture, Smallville UK, Mr wet underpants 1989, Death Valley Amusements and 10 pints of frogspawn. To the court of St James - there's a view of any train pulling through the backstreets of any Northern town calling you a liar. By the tomb of the unknown shopper another lorry dumps 2 tons of ear wax on the wrong lawn and a fat tongue comes on the radio, it says 'sorry but. . sorry but . . sorry but . . (click).

At the end of your clean clothes chain in anorak, tank top, shorts and odd socks, on the way to the launderette you say you're just trying to get through, but is it ever enough just to get through? To the court of St James - there's blood on your pages. I can almost see the stains on the white white cliffs as we near the coast of the poem I hope I shall never write called England

A GIFT

At 7 o'clock this morning
I bring you a mountain
I tap gently on your window
and you wake half covered in sleep.

"What's that?" you ask
"It's a mountain" I grin,
"I've carried it all night
I couldn't sleep so I brought it
here to show you."
"What do I want with a mountain in my garden at 7 o'clock in the
morning?" you ask, not used to being woken at 7 o'clock with a
mountain in your garden.

I try to joke, now feeling a little embarrassed,
"It's for you, a gift."
You say you don't want a mountain.
You are too tired to understand,
and I struggle to explain it's not the mountain I've brought you
it's the fact that I could bring it to you.
I strain to pick it up again and wonder what I'm going to do with it now.
I feel such a fool walking home with a mountain.

HOW THE YOUNG AND FASHIONABLE ARE FEELING THIS SEASON

They're wearing their
consciences well hid
this season. Hearts on
the sleeve are definitely
out. Compassion's out.
Basically the effect is not
to distract attention
from the expensive clothes.

SEX BEFORE PARENTS

A parent expects
their son to have sex
but not so their daughter
true values they've taught her.

But with their double standard logic
they never seem to have thought of
the fact their son sleeps around
with other parent's daughters.

LIKE BOB HOPE AND BING CROSBY IN "ROAD TO PUBERTY"

When I was 15 I used to have a friend,
he was my best friend..............and I hated him.
He had perfect teeth
and he always won on the slot machines
just after I'd been on and lost;
he was my best friend...........and I hated him.
He was a little older than me
so I used to tell his girlfriends
his teeth were false.
When they kissed him they'd try and lick the inside of
his gums and he'd think they were being sexy.
I told them he wore a toupee as well
and they'd run their fingers through his hair
and he'd smile away – the daft bastard.
He was better than me at everything
but he was my best friend..............and I hated him.
And I hated myself for hating him
which made me hate him even more.
I'd call him sanctimonious –
and he'd forgive me.
It's said you like people for their good points
but you love them for their faults
and he never had any faults –
apart that is from his choice of best friend,
and for that I suppose I loved him.

SUZANNE

She's never come to terms with her shape
or been comfortable with any of her hairstyles

the clothes she hangs herself in never hold the person
she feels she wants to see in the mirror

no matter how she sits she feels awkward
she doesn't like the summer, it casts shadows on her face

she says her face is too angular that's the problem
tight fitting clothes make her feel disproportionate

she never looks how she feels
maybe she's getting old, she thinks.

WHEN HOMES BECOME HOUSES

You can't be too careful these days
now love is riddled with herpes
and crippled with A.I.D.S.
So I've taken to wearing a durex over my head, just in case.

I've put a durex over the cat
a durex over the car
and although it reduces sensitivity
it makes perfect sense to me
last night I put a durex over my heart

Love is,
            now a durex bed with durex pillows
we live in a durex house with nailed down windows
we speak only through sanitized phones, durex extra safe
and we want to be buried in a six foot durex, in separate graves.

INTERNAL MEMO

Forget big business

the only holding company
I want
is you

THE MUTUALLY ASSURED DESTRUCTION OF MR. AND MRS. JONE

Like most arguments neither can remember who fired the first shot.
Both still had snipers positioned from their previous confrontations.
Both had started to build entrenchments. This time though it had
escalated into open conflict on a scale never seen before.
Mr. Jones was flexing his muscles.
Mr. Jones was about to demonstrate who wore the trousers.
Mrs. Jones was beating the shit out of him.
In the aftermath there followed a period of chilled silence.
This Mr. and Mrs. Jones referred to as the cold war.
They built a wall between them. At first friends dropped in supplies.
Each began developing new weapons to inflict pain upon the other.
Each labelled their weapons "deterrents."
Each was determined if need be to "deterrent" the other into oblivion.
Then gradually as paranoia became a firm enough basis to build upon
peace talks began.
But if one day either of their tongues should slip....

THE REFLECTION IN THE BACK OF GOD'S SPOON

Nude modelling for the afterlife
she secures the burger concession in Paradise

It's difficult to be concerned at the world's wrongs
with an industrial base of cream scones

There's an empty funhouse with a formica carousel
A gardener nurturing humanity on the high road to Hell

Originality for the mass market reaped with a vengeance
individually wrapped tears and brutal indifference

As reproach stalks this poetry in thin disguise
for dogs bound by pavement there is little pride

All the seas of Mercy yet to understand
I feel the sadness of computers in an enchanted land

How can the Mortician fill dead bodies with formaldehyde
then go home and make love to his wife?

The wasting of limbs and the squandering of belief
Perpetual emotion and the dignity of trees
It's fear of death
beating the wings of my heart
I reach for your hand in the dark
I reach for your hand in the dark

THE FIRST FRACTURE OF INNOCENCE IS THE HATCHING OF ALL REGRET

Ours is a strange love affair
The only Magpie left to mourn
    is phantom upon my back

His song laments his long lost mate
He tells me he will cling to me even in dreams
He will circle my burial
    even as the prayers fall away
He will brood forever over my scratch of earth

For ours is a strange love affair
    yet without his faith in instinct
who else could understand how sweet were once
    the purest notes of joy

Imperfection itself should grieve
    to have suffocated such a tiny breath
no parchment can ever dress this wound
or weeping ever wash even the smallest regret from the land
Death is a burden clasped on every back

And ours is a strange love affair
Punishment to shame remorse
Sorrow already perched on an empty grave

TRAVELLING SECOND CLASS THROUGH HOPE

With softer spine you rise and shine
And strap yourself safe in time
More beads for the natives, more gongs for the troops,
You buy off the kids with spaghetti hoops
Melt into the monotone, the drip-feed TV
Death Wish 4, Funland UK, until you say
Is this all there is ?

You say you need a cause, you need to fight
You're looking for something, anything
If only you had something noble denied
You say sometimes you'd fight everything
So down at the beast market
You seek solace in your crisps
Hey what's a nice Jaeger jumper like that
Doing in a place like this?
You see Madonna singing "Material Girl"
To earthquake victims in The Third World
You see a white car drive through Soweto
Swords designed as shields
The new credit card diplomacy
And the worship of God on wheels, and you say
Is this all there is ?

And when the party's over, and limp lettuce and lager trodden into the carpet are no longer part of the fun. And you realise that the Earth doesn't revolve around three pubs in the centre of town. And you realise your God's not bigger than my God after all. Travelling second class through Hope, you pray, there must be more than this.

THE LADIES' MAN

He poured the word darling like acid
It ate
Through
Nameless
Women
Faceless
As the acid
Scoured
The flesh
From the bone
Darling – it smarted, keen to the touch
Darling – it stung, as it seeped into the conversation
He poured the darling like acid
Saying "Don't worry your pretty little head now
Don't worry your pretty little head."

PRAGMATIC ROMANTICISM

1. . . .for want of a better word we call it love.

With your leg bent over mine I can feel the moistness of your desire.
With your breast cupped against my lifeline I can feel the
flourish of your heart.
There is a dance within your pulse.

2. Some days I lie in bed all morning waiting for the phone to ring.

I could get up but I need outside intervention. Some stimulus, catalyst,
impetus. the door bell to buzz, the landlord to knock, the window cleaner
to bruise his ladders against the paintwork, a poster to fall from the
wall, the bedroom to burst into flames, anything.
I am already dead, my carcass exhumed to imitate devotion
Some days I close my eyes and lay my heart off the hook.

3. Acceptance being the onset of maturity
3. responsibility, the irritant, dissolves into static.

3. Once. Maybe.
3. On another continent
3. where the sky seemed wider
3. allowing arms to stretch out and loosen the joints.
There
without fear of declaring our love
we held hands across a culture
like two mirrors turned inwards
reflecting a private eternity.
If there is no such thing as true love then all logic is built
on the smallest unit of time.

THE ACCIDENTAL DEATH OF A CAT

Outside the polling office
I saw a cat that had never voted
run over by a man made machine
that failed to notice

Like a circus crowd
a random cross-section of the electorate
as if being entertained by a performing poodle
spectated, as spasms of pain
jerked the body into acrobatics.

Someone went to phone . . but to phone who?
Someone went to find the owner.
Someone went for a half brick.

the cat lay still at last, one eye dangling loose
like a battered old teddy bear.
The half brick was discarded.
The cat placed reverently into a Safeways carrier bag.

The afternoon sun dried the small smudges of blood
into the tarmac.
The colours meshed so that soon you
could hardly notice the difference
when you passed.
Later that night all parties claimed victory.

THE SONG

While
some people
find joy
humming along
to the enchanting music of the song

Others
listen closely
to the words
trying to comprehend
the true meaning of the song

but sadly
not all the words are audible

THE LAST POEM I EVER WROTE

The last poem I ever wrote I had such high hopes for.
The last poem I ever wrote was to have been so powerful it would make
war obsolete and nuclear fusion as vital as trainspotting. It was to
have been so cleverly constructed it would hold the key to the
very universe itself, make Arthur C. Clarke redundant and James Burke
intelligible; so full of life it would be strapped onto wounds, and made
into tablets and ointment. The Olympic committee would disqualify
competitors found to have read it. Laid over the face of a child's corpse
it would bring the dead back to life.
The last poem I ever wrote was published in a low budget poetry
magazine boasting a print run of 220, 150 of which still remain under
the editor's bed. The title escapes me but it was some pathetic pun
such as "Write Now."
The last poem I ever wrote was performed to an alternative cabaret
audience at Cleethorpes off-season in between an alternative juggler and
a 22-piece Catalonian dance band. Coinciding with the call for last
orders it was heckled constantly by a drunk born and bred in London who
sang in a scotch accent and claimed to own the city of Glasgow
personally.
The last poem I ever wrote was entered in a poetry competition by a
lifelong enemy. The judges having been certified dead were suitably
appointed as their names were unknown even to each other let alone to
anyone else. My poem came 63rd out of 7 million entries and won a
year's subscription to the Crumpsall Poetry Appreciation Society
Crochet Circle and Glee Club Gazette.
The last poem I ever wrote was cremated along with my body, unread.
The last poem I ever wrote was carried in the hearts of those I loved.

St VALENTINE'S DAY RESTS NOT ON THE CALENDER BUT IN THE HEART

(Her eyes were emerald and there was a simple joy in watching)
her brush her hair)

As if bewitched by childhood
I have seen you dazzle
I have lightened my frown to the bond of sweethearts
I have chanced the whirlwind of derision
And as childhood ends
on yet another train I cower from
Chinese whispers that taunt floodlights on my illusions
New friends tell me I've become disfigured in repartee
that all softness or aggression is passe
that detachment is sophistication
To think it should come to this
To think it should come to this

. . .sometimes I wonder if I've ever been in love
it's like trying to explain why a joke is funny

No matter how I faint indifference, I still fear flying.
As each plane leaves the ground my prayers are of you.
If the soul survives I want above all to hold your presence
This may not weigh heavy in the glib torrent of conversation
but at times such as these the dead do not lie, not to themselves

I realise to you I am already fable
It seems I lost you even before we met
. . .don't look at me now I've grown old and ugly whilst you remain
breathless as a new constellation

SORRY

"Sorry" is a small word only five letters
that is four different letters and one swap
having two letter 'r's.

"I love you" is three small words
eight letters, that is seven and one swap
the letter 'o'.

"I forgive you" is two small words and a fairly
small word, eleven letters, ten and one swap.

I'll exchange you one of my most valuable
"sorry's" and an almost priceless "I love you"
that's thirteen letters in all, if you say
"I forgive you."

Of course, if you want to throw in an "I love you too,"
we can really start talking business.

OTHER BOOKS BY HENRY NORMAL NOW IN PRINT -

from

A TWIST IN THE TALE PUBLICATIONS
18 HIND ST., RETFORD, NOTTS. DN22 7EN

Is love science fiction? -

A5 booklet, 48 pages, glossy cover, bound.
Update of first collection of Love poems.
Price £2.30 (inc. p&p)

Love Like Hell -

A5 booklet, 36 pages, glossy cover, bound.
Second collection of love poems.
Price £2.30 (inc. p&p)

Does inflation affect the emotions? -

A5 booklet, 40 pages, glossy cover, bound.
Third collection of love poems.
Price £2.30 (inc p&p)

The Outer Limits of Henry Normal -

A5 booklet, 36 pages, glossy cover, bound.
Short comic stories, illustrated.
Price £2.30 (inc p&p)

BOOKS BY PAUL COOKSON

"Funny, direct and has a conscience. This poetry demands a response."

STRAIT MAGAZINE

Unclench the Fists -

A4, 40 pages, card cover, stapled.
Collection of performance poems.
Price £1.50 (incl. p&p)

Sketches -

A5, 28 pages, glossy cover, stapled.
Short poems with a personal touch.
Price £1.50 (incl. p&p).

Batman and Oddy -

A5 book, 48 pages, 4 colour glossy cover, bound. Poems and short stories entering the world of Oddy at desk high level. Artwork by Cliff Woodcock, Introduction by Mike Harding.
Price £2.95 (incl. p&p).

The Amazing Captain Concorde -

Illustrated collection of poetry for children.
Price £3.95 (incl. p&p).

Over 21 and Still into Noddy -

Selected poems 1979 - 1990
Introduction by Noddy Holder.
Price £4.95 (incl p&p).

Available from:
A TWIST IN THE TALE, 18 Hind St., Retford, Notts. DN22 7EN.
Tel: 0777 700248
Please make all cheques and postal orders payable to "A Twist in the Tale"

TYPESET & PRINTED
BY
THE BOOK PRESS
Telephone (0602) 459405

The Book Press is a subsidiary of Kenworthy Trading Ltd., Nottingham,
who print most of the books for A Twist in the Tale Publications
and who could at a pinch probably print for you too.